Essence

Essence: *365 God Thoughts About You*

This book is set in the typeface *Athelas* designed by Veronika Burian and Jose Scaglione.
Editor: Elizabeth Maynard Charlé – Polish Point Editing
Cover Design and Typesetting: Tall Pine Books
Cover Art: *Victory's Ride* by Artist: Rebekah Jo Leebens

Hardcover ISBN: 978-1-955546-54-6
Paperback ISBN: 978-1-955546-53-9

A Publication of *Tall Pine Books*
119 E Center Street, Suite B4A | Warsaw, Indiana 46580
www.tallpinebooks.com

| 1 23 23 20 16 02 |

Published in the United States of America

Essence

365 God Thoughts about You

Christine Tracy

Foreword by
Ray Hughes

Endorsements

Essence - 365 God Thoughts about You by Christine Tracy is a beacon of light and a source of unwavering inspiration. This book is a testament to the author's remarkable ability to capture the essence of spirituality, hope, and the boundless goodness of God in every single day.

Christine Tracy, a seasoned blogger and coach for aspiring authors, has embarked on a remarkable journey of transformation with this book. Drawing from her years of experience and her deep well of wisdom, she has meticulously crafted a collection of God-inspired thoughts, poetry, and prose that will undoubtedly touch the hearts and souls of readers.

Essence is not just a book; it's a daily companion on a spiritual voyage. With 365 thought-provoking entries, each day offers a fresh perspective, a new revelation, and a reminder of the divine presence in our lives. Tracy's words are like a gentle whisper from the heavens, providing solace, strength, and a renewed sense of purpose to those who seek it. With each page, she encourages us to embrace our unique purpose and potential, igniting a flame within us that can brighten not only our own lives but the lives of those around us.

Essence - 365 God Thoughts about You is a treasure trove of inspiration, a daily dose of spiritual nourishment, and a testament to the goodness that resides within each of us.

Christine Tracy's book is a gift to humanity, a reminder that in the midst of life's challenges, we can always find solace, guidance, and grace in the presence of God.

I wholeheartedly endorse this book and believe it will become a cherished companion for anyone seeking to deepen their spiritual connection and live a life filled with purpose, hope, and the goodness of God.

—Dr. Brian Simmons, *Passion & Fire Ministries*
Lead Translator of *The Passion Translation*

Chris Tracy will awaken the wonder of life's many precious moments that can sneak past us because we are so busy trudging through life without learning to look up. If you want to be awakened to the beauty of God's creation and the gifts God gives you every day, then look no further because you will find it in Chris' devotional, *Essence.*

I have known Chris through her being one of my students at Bethel School of Supernatural Ministry and now as a student and partner in my online Create Academy, and I believe her heart for God and the wonder of encounters with God have found their home in these pages. Get this book and put it by your Bible and dive into a great adventure of knowing the essence of love.

—Theresa Dedmon
Create Academy Founder and Director

Essence, what a perfect title for this book because the heart of the writer has creatively designed for the reader something to experience the thoughts of God on a daily basis. Each day, Christine opens a door into a wonderland of words that move the soul into a place where promises come true. The author does not flip a coin to decide which scripture she will use, but with deep thought and expectancy, the gifted writer discovers the right message for those who hunger for God. In the end, it feels like God and the writer are working together to inspire and revive the reader's heart.

—Don Milam Jr.
Words Create Worlds
Acquisitions Consultant, Coach, and Writer

I've known Chris as someone who can see God in every turn in the road, and glorious possibilities in every situation. She blends the Word of God, her experiences, and the beauties of nature into short daily meditations that are enriching and fortifying. I encourage you to make these meditations a regular companion for your daily living.

—Frank Frantz
Author of: Lord of the Harvest
World Shakers, and *Daniel, God's Bondservant*

Reading Christine Tracy's *Essence* each day will bring fresh perspective to your morning. I love how she sees the mundane things of life, but through her intuitive lens, confronts the ordinary, transforming it into extraordinary adventure. As you read each day's thought, focus on God's peace and may His serenity enfold you.

—Elizabeth M. Charlé
Author and Editor

Learning to renew our minds according to God's Word is one of the most powerful tools God gives us in our transformation journey. I'm thankful Chris has written this devotional to help us all come to know what God thinks about us, according to His Word.

—Matt Tommey
www.MattTommeyMentoring.com

If you're looking for a way to start your day on the bright side, you'll love Chris Tracy's devotional, *Essence: 365 God Thoughts about You*. When I read these daily "rays of Sonshine," I see the words of a beautiful soul expressing God's heart for us, paired with scripture verses, that impart joy, encouragement, and wise spiritual insight. If you're experiencing a cloudy, rainy, or dark day, step into the *Essence* of *God's Thoughts About You*, and see from heaven's perspective, a glorious day ahead!

—PJ Clark
Author of Warrior Dance - From Darkness to Glory
www.desertthunderarts.com

When I was a kid, growing up, I remember spending the night at my grandparents' house. What made these times so special was sitting at the kitchen counter in the morning, watching my grandma adeptly prepare some of the best breakfasts in the world. I can still sense the smell of bacon, biscuits, gravy, home-fries, and fried eggs wafting through my memories, as I would listen to my grandma go on and on about adventurous journeys of the past, sharing all of the wisdom she gained in doing life with Jesus, her family, and friends from Church through them all.

But the best treat was always the way my grandma would sow into me such positive and hopeful insights about how God could help me in my life. From time to time, I still find myself wishing that I could sit at that kitchen counter with her every morning, hearing more of the things that only a grandma can poor into our legacy.

As I read through, *Essence*, I couldn't help but imagine sitting at the breakfast counter with Chris Tracy every morning, and getting the encouragement and insights that would help me get through the challenges of life, as well as fulfilling my God-given destiny.

Essence is a simple book, but like my grandma, Chris has an amazing way of making profound truths, simple. If you are looking for some breakfast time with a grandma of the Faith, then this book is a must. It's not just a book; it's a spiritual breakfast, that will nourish you throughout your adventurous journey.

—Kevin Dedmon
Author, Conference Speaker, Revivalist
The Ultimate Treasure Hunt, Unlocking Heaven, The Risk Factor, Firestarters, Gnosticized, Presence Therapy

Chris Tracy has a unique ability to condense powerful truths into bite-sized pieces. She is a great friend for those who may not have a lot of time to read but still want a daily injection of truth and hope. She has certainly done this in her powerful book, *Essence.* Through her wonderful insights, you will be encouraged every day of the year with a scriptural truth to live out for that day. In every devotional teaching, you will find yourself filled with increased hope, vision for the future, and purpose in your identity. I highly recommend this book to you.

—Steve Backlund
Co-Founder of *Igniting Hope Ministries*

I've trusted Chris and her discernment of what God is up to ever since I met her and Rick. Chris is a trustworthy, honoring and relevant spiritual leader. She brings great experience and leadership to the table in everything she does, and her latest book is no exception. If you are looking to grow closer to the Lord and in your identity as a son/daughter of the Most High, this book will be a great resource for you.

—Jeremy Brown
CEO, *Throne Publishing Group*
thronepg.com

To my greatest encourager, my husband, Rick Tracy. Your patience, love, humor, and sense of adventure made us perfect life mates. Thanks for being a pioneer with me. I love you.

Contents

Foreword

Today, if you ask ten people their thoughts about God, I bet you'd get a hundred answers. Some of those answers would be confusing, contradictory, and outright bewildering. Chris has given us 365 excellent reminders that His thoughts toward us are far more beautiful than ours toward Him. Thank you, God, and thank you, Chris.

—Ray Hughes
Author, Poet, Storyteller, Teacher
rayhughes.org

Preface

In 2015 I gave myself an assignment to post an encouraging word every day to my blog, Crisp Mountain Air (www.crispmountainair.blogspot.com) I would sit outside my Colorado home and ask God for a word for each specific date and write down the first thing that would come into my mind. It was usually an image, a thought, or something I noticed in my yard like a bird or a flower. I would dig further, asking Him what He wanted to say. Then I'd write something brief, find a Bible verse or quote that went with it, and post it to my blog with one of my photos. This was no small task to stay the course for a whole year. But I did, and even now refer to those posts on particular days, encouraging myself for the day.

After years of blogging and coaching authors, I felt compelled to begin to put my blogposts, poetry, and prose into books. My prayer is for you to be brightened every day the same way sunshine warms your face on a mountain morning. You are called to be a breath of fresh air to a weary, fearful world, hungry to know the God in you – the hope of glory.

Thank you for reading my book. May it strengthen and bless each day.

Love,
Chris

January

January

January 1 - Fulfilled Promises

In Colorado, winter's snow and year-round sunshine ensure a brilliant crop of wildflowers in the exquisite mountain summer. Know that this winter interlude is giving birth to a brilliant delivery of fulfilled promises, fresh hope, new life, new opportunity, unexpected prosperity, and answers from our good Papa God.

Jeremiah 29:11 - "For I know the plans I have for you," declares the Lord, "plans to prosper you and not to harm you, plans to give you hope and a future." (NIV)

January 2 - It's an Overcoming Day

Many go through the holiday season recalling past hurts. Today is a day to overcome; to let go of the shock, despair, and depression. Today is God's day of victory in your life.

It's time to climb out into the sunshine of a new day, a new year, and the rest of your life. You can do it. God is with you and He will help you.

John 1:5 - The light shines in the darkness, and the darkness has not overcome it. (NIV)

~

January 3 - Interlude

Interlude. What a poetic word. I feel God's love on this word today, asking us to take an interlude—a space in time, a moment in our day to be with Him. Take a walk. Turn off the noise. Quiet your spirit. Just be. He will fill that interlude with Himself in your life.

Psalm 46:10 - "Be still and know that I am God." (NIV)

~

January 4 - Watch for Those "But God" Moments

We have all suffered shock and trauma if we have lived on this Earth very long. The enemy of our souls would love to use that to harm us more, keeping us from healing and from our destiny. But God. Do you know there are "but God" moments throughout the Bible? God always has a better plan. In moments of our greatest weakness, God still invades. We only need to reach for His hand. He will pull us out.

Psalm 73:26 - My flesh and my heart may fail, but God is the strength of my heart and my portion forever. (NIV)

January 5 - A Joyful Morning to You

Joyful mornings are yours starting today. Bright sunrises yield warm thoughts of God's promises. God has a promise for every situation. Did you know that? Ask Him to show you—then position yourself to learn His promises for you today.

Psalms 30:5: - ... weeping may stay for the night, but rejoicing comes in the morning. (NIV)

Psalms 30:11 - You turned my wailing into dancing; you removed my sackcloth and clothed me with joy. (NIV)

2 Corinthians 1:20 - For no matter how many promises God has made, they are "Yes" in Christ. And so through him the "Amen" is spoken by us to the glory of God. (NIV)

January 6 - God Really Wants You to Know Him

Do you know that God is relational? He sent his son, Jesus, so we could know how to relate to the Father. Sometimes I picture myself at an old, rustic table, drinking great wine in the company of Jesus, God, and Holy Spirit. It's family time at its best. Today, He wants you to find Him this way—as a loving Father longing for His child to know Him ... to really *know* Him.

John 10:27 – "My own sheep will hear my voice and I know each one, and they will follow me." (TPT)

~

January 7 - Move That Mountain

What mountain or giant have you been facing that is daring you to conquer it? Today is a day of breakthrough. Take that step and overcome. Fears, crises, challenges, financial issues, job difficulties, and life changes—they will all bow today to your authority as you take that step.

Matthew 17:20 – "Truly I tell you, if you have faith as small as a mustard seed, you can say to this mountain, 'Move from here to there,' and it will move. Nothing will be impossible for you." (NIV)

~

January 8 - Energy for Change

The holidays are over. Christmas decorations are packed away, and thoughts of spring cleaning take shape along with creative ideas for new things in your life. Take a breath of that crisp mountain air. Let it fill your lungs, blood cells, and brain cells. Energy for change can be yours today. Grab hold—it belongs to you!

Job 33:4 - The Spirit of God has made me; the breath of the Almighty gives me life. (NIV)

~

January 9 - The Gift of Exhilaration

Bright blue sky against a glistening blanket of fresh snow is a present to the soul. God has prepared this day for you to enjoy in nature and in the spirit. What exhilarates you? Be aware of that gift to you today.

James 1:17 - Every good and perfect gift is from above, coming down from the Father of the heavenly lights, who does not change like shifting shadows. (NIV)

~

January 10 - Speak Life

If your day looks difficult, declare it easy. If it looks long with problems, declare it bright with promise. If it looks bad, declare it good. Look for the hope, joy, and blessings in every day. When we practice hope, it attracts good things. When we practice hopelessness, it attracts negative things. You can turn things around. Practice hope, and it will help others do the same.

Psalm 4:6 - Many people say, "Who will show us better times?" Let your face smile on us, Lord. (NLT)

Mark 11:23 – "Truly I tell you, if anyone says to this mountain, 'Go, throw yourself into the sea,' and does not doubt in their heart but believes that what they say will happen, it will be done for them." (NIV)

~

January 11 - Miraculous Life

In the mountains there is a natural phenomenon called alpenglow. At sundown in winter, on very cold, clear evenings, a precious rosy glow colors the snowy peaks. Peace fills my soul when I witness this, as it helps me remember there is so much more to life than my immediate worries. Like the alpenglow, your life is a miracle that helps someone else see their life differently.

Genesis 2:7 - Then the Lord God formed a man from the dust of the ground and breathed into his nostrils the breath of life, and the man became a living being. (NIV)

~

January 12 - Love

God wants you to know today how much He loves you. Look up. Let Him fill your entire being. Watch for a new promise He has for you regarding relationships in your life.

Ephesians 3:19 - And to know this love that surpasses knowledge - that you may be filled to the measure of all the fullness of God. (NIV)

~

January 13 - Witness God's Protection

God protects you always, but by being more mindful of His presence, you will notice and witness this protection today and in the days ahead. Stay close to Him, remembering He is close to you every moment. Then, you will not have to suffer worry or stress.

Psalm 46:1 - God is our refuge and strength, a very present help in trouble. (NIV)

~

January 14 - Be Aware

Just as our wireless generation communicates through a "space" dimension, and just as the wind blows and we know it's there because we feel it, but can't see it, so is our spiritual life a reality. Be aware. Things are happening in the Spirit today, and if you pay attention, you will sense it.

John 3:8 - The wind blows wherever it pleases. You hear its sound, but you cannot tell where it comes from or where it is going. So it is with everyone born of the Spirit. (NIV)

January 15 - Tell Your Stories

Chances are you worry about your family members and their faith. Do you know that your stories of how God blesses you will always build their beliefs? In the Bible it happened again and again. Simple stories led a family, a household, and even a whole town to believe. Just tell your stories. God did not make it hard for His kids to find Him. He loves you so much. He is a good Father.

John 4:53 - Then the father realized that this was the exact time at which Jesus had said to him, "Your son will live." So he and his whole household believed. (NASB)

Acts 11:14 - He will bring you a message through which you and all your household will be saved. (NLT)

January 16 - Listen

There is a sound that brings you deeper ... deeper into beauty, love, joy, and peace. It could be music, the sound of a brook, or a baby's coo. It could be thunder or thundering waves. It could be the song of a bird or the voice of your true love. Today, revel in that kind of sound, and it will bring you healing and peace.

Revelation 19:6 - Then I heard what sounded like a great multitude, like the roar of rushing waters and like loud peals of thunder, shouting "Hallelujah!" For our Lord God Almighty reigns. (NIV)

~

January 17 - "I AM"

Do you know that God has lots of names? Some of them mean: "I am the light of the world; I am your provider; I am your healer; I am your comfort; I am your rock and your salvation; I am your hope. Father, papa, daddy, friend." Oh, how His heart breaks when we think of Him as distant and someone to fear to the point of running and hiding. Today, take a step closer to your Papa God, and you will begin to know Him by one of His wonderful names.

Psalm 148:13 - Let them praise the name of the Lord, for his name alone is exalted; his splendor is above the earth and the heavens. (NIV)

~

January 18 - Time for Trust

God has already given us all of Him. He only asks for all of us. Only in that relationship can we realize the love, gifts, protection, trust, assurance, and blessings He wants to give us. It's easy to give ourselves totally to someone who loves us completely. Just say "yes" to Him. Just believe. Let Him know you can't do it alone anymore. Whisper, "I need you, Lord. Please take over my life. I trust you completely." He will hear you and will answer.

Proverbs 3:5-6 - Trust in the Lord with all your heart and lean not on your own understanding; in all your ways submit to him, and he will make your paths straight. (NIV)

~

January 19 - Trips and Surprises

Today is a day for planning. Good trips are ahead of you with more surprises than you realize. Make that reservation, and make those phone calls today.

Psalm 20:4 – May he give you the desire of your heart and make all your plans succeed. (NIV)

~

January 20 - Truth: You Are Getting Better

You are getting stronger and growing better as a person. Do you see that happening? Probably not. But God wants you to know you are doing great. He is so proud of you and the person you are becoming. Today, you will see beyond the trials and problems, and grab hold of the truth that they are making you better.

James 1:2 - My brethren, count it all joy when you fall into various trials, knowing that the testing of your faith produces patience. But let patience have its perfect work, that you may be perfect and complete, lacking nothing. (NKJV)

~

January 21 - Arise! Shine!

You are a bright light in a dark world. There are people around you who are drawn to that light, and it will help them. You are learning to recognize that light in others, too. It's a day and a time to shine.

Isaiah 60:1 - Arise, shine, for your light has come, and the glory of the Lord rises upon you. (NIV)

~

January 22 - You Have a Helper

You have a helper. Today He will be there, right with you, as you face something you thought you couldn't handle. But you will. You will handle it, and you will be amazed at the result.

Philippians 4:13 - I can do all things through Christ who strengthens me. (NKJV)

Philippians 4:12-13 - I know what it means to lack, and I know what it means to experience overwhelming abundance. For I'm trained in the secret of overcoming all things, whether in fullness or in hunger. And I find that the strength of

Christ's explosive power infuses me to conquer every difficulty. (TPT)

~

January 23 - You Will Overcome

Do you ever feel "under"—under the weather, underappreciated, less than? It's a bad place fraught with weakness, despair, and self-pity. Instead of feeling "under," try turning that around to have an opposite effect. Declare yourself "over!" You are healthy, strong, smart, on top of things, and embracing the truth that God appreciates you. You are an overcomer.

John 16:33 - "I have told you these things, so that in me you may have peace. In this world you will have trouble. But take heart! I have overcome the world." (NIV)

~

January 24 - Heavenly Oil

Do you ever feel irritated—ready to lash out, give up, or stomp away from a situation? Take a deep breath, then find a Psalm or a poetic passage, and read it more than once. Read it aloud. Imagine an oil of peace flowing over you as you read. That heavenly oil has power in it to help you see from a different perspective.

In Jesus' famous reading of Isaiah 61 (see verses 1-3), he talked about this oil, identifying himself as the one who would *"bestow on them a crown of beauty instead of ashes, the oil of joy instead of mourning, and a garment of praise instead of a spirit of despair."* He said of us: *"They will be called oaks of righteousness, a planting of the Lord for the display of his splendor." (NIV)*

~

January 25 · A Good Kind of Hungry

Jesus often spoke of hunger—both physical and spiritual. We are in a good place when we hunger for more of God. As you seek and pray to know Him more, He is releasing more wisdom, love, and beauty into your life than you could ever imagine.

Psalm 34:8 – Taste and see that the Lord is good; blessed is the one who takes refuge in him. (NIV)

~

January 26 · God Holds Your Hand

In winter, the elk herd near where we live gathers in our neighborhood, eating and bedding down in meadows of dry grass. They know they are safe in this area. There are no hunters, and laws protect them in this season. Like those elk, you want to gather your loved ones and feel safe, protected by something more powerful than you. That something—that someone—is God. And He is right there.

Psalm 73:23 - Yet I am always with you; you hold me by my right hand. (NIV)

Matthew 1:23 - "...and they will call him Immanuel" (which means "God with us." (NIV)

~

January 27 - Power to Accomplish Much

There is extra power in this day for you to get lots done that is on your to-do list. Do you know that what matters to you matters to God? Go over your list with him, then expect supernatural help, wisdom, and guidance as you check off each task and finish your day in victory.

Proverbs 8:14 - Counsel and sound judgment are mine; I have insight, I have power. (NIV)

~

January 28 – A Quiet Walk

God walked with Adam in the cool of the day, and they enjoyed each other's company as friends. That's how God wants to relate to you. Reach out your hand and feel your hand in His today. Just enjoy Him. Converse as friends and rest in His presence.

Proverbs 18:24 – There is a friend who sticks closer than a brother. (NIV)

John 15:15 – "I have never called you 'servants,' because a master doesn't confide in his servants, and servants don't always understand what the master is doing. But I call you my most intimate and cherished friends, for I reveal to you everything that I've heard from my Father." (TPT)

~

January 29 - It's Okay to Be Happy

Jesus was the happiest person in history. Many of us have been taught of His holiness, parables, miracles, and gift of salvation. But we haven't been taught a lot about His joy. The Kingdom of God is made up of righteousness, peace, and joy. Joy makes up a third of the Kingdom. God laughs. Jesus joyfully loves. Even King David danced in celebration. Today brings a new realm of joy ... even silly joy. Kids know how to do this well. Today, you will know, too. Let go and have joy.

Romans 14:17 - For the kingdom of God is not a matter of eating and drinking, but of righteousness, peace, and joy in the Holy Spirit. (NIV)

Hebrews 1:9 - "Therefore God, Your God, has anointed You with the oil of gladness more than Your companions." (NKJV)

~

January 30 - Nature Watch

Trees and bushes will begin to show signs of life soon. Branches will begin to turn color and thicken. Buds will begin to form on limbs. The earth is getting ready to take a deep breath. The turn of the month affects your spirit in a good way. Breathe deep and revel in the peace that nature is bringing.

Psalm 42:2 – My soul thirsts, pants, and longs for the living God. I want to come and see the face of God. (TPT)

~

January 31 – Provision and Protection

There is a fresh, new beginning that starts today and continues through the next several months. You are ready. Provision and protection are yours from your Father in Heaven.

Ephesians 3:20 - God can do anything, you know - far more than you could ever imagine or guess or request in your wildest dreams! He does it not by pushing us around but by working within us, his Spirit deeply and gently within us. (MSG)

February

February

February 1 - God Is Revealing His Secrets to You

Precious moments of silence are like sweet treats to your soul. You are finding those moments more often when you sit and rest. Find freedom and hear the whispers from Heaven. Secrets are being revealed.

Proverbs 25:2 - God conceals the revelation of His Word in the hiding place of His glory. But the honor of kings is revealed to all by how they thoroughly mine out the deeper meaning of all that God says. (TPT)

~

February 2 - The Beauty of Holiness

What is the beauty of holiness? It's not being dressed in suits and ties, dresses and finery, and going to church for an hour a week. Instead, it's the sweet presence created in time spent with your Creator. He thinks you are beautiful —every moment—no matter how you look, what you do, or where you are.

Psalm 96:9 - Oh, worship the Lord in the beauty of holiness! Tremble before Him, all the earth. (NKJV)

February 3 - Trust God for Your Outcome

With decks of cards and games of chance, we can't know the outcome. Our life is like that. Fear keeps us from walking toward our destiny because we can't be sure of our outcome. God wants us to take those steps and trust Him for the outcome. It is our demonstration of this faith that so pleases Him.

Hebrews 11:1 - Now faith is the substance of things hoped for, the evidence of things not seen. (NKJV)

Hebrews 11:6 - And without faith it is impossible to please God, because anyone who comes to him must believe that he exists and that he rewards those who earnestly seek him. (NIV)

February 4 - Listen to a Child's Words

Spend some time with a child today, and listen for how God will talk to you through them.

Matthew 18:10 - "See that you do not despise one of these little ones. For I tell you that their angels in heaven always see the face of my Father in heaven." (NIV)

Matthew 19:14 - Jesus said, "Let the little children come to me, and do not hinder them, for the kingdom of heaven belongs to such as these." (NIV)

February 5 - Strength from Heaven

Like manna from Heaven, much is being released to you right now that will sustain you and give you strength.

Psalm 28:7 - The Lord is my strength and my shield; my heart trusts in him, and he helps me. (NIV)

February 6 - Be Kind and Be Blessed

Show someone kindness today through words and actions. That person will be blessed and so will you.

1 Peter 3:8-9 - Finally, all of you, be like-minded, be sympathetic, love one another, be compassionate and humble. Do not repay evil with evil or insult with insult. On the contrary, repay evil with blessing, because to this you were called so that you may inherit a blessing. (NIV)

February 7 - It's All About the Love

If you are introverted, extend love to a stranger today. If you are extroverted, slow down enough to truly listen to a friend.

1 John 4:12 - No one has ever seen God; but if we love one another, God lives in us and his love is made complete in us. (NIV)

~

February 8 - Words Just for You

Read today in the book of Psalms and watch words and passages jump out—highlighted as if they are a direct word to you from the Author— which they are. God's Word gives life.

Psalm 90:14 - Let our dark night end and the sunrise of Your love break through our clouded dawn again! Only You can satisfy our hearts, filling us with songs of joy and gladness to the end of our days. Come and restore us! (TPT)

~

February 9 - Compelled for Success

You are compelled to do something today, and it will succeed. Those compulsions, if they are good, are from the Holy Spirit. It's a way He talks to us, so listen closely.

Habakkuk 2:14 - For the earth will be filled with the knowledge of the glory of the Lord as the waters cover the sea. (NKJV)

Philippians 4:8-9 - Summing it all up, friends, I'd say you'll do best by filling your minds and meditating on things true, noble, reputable, authentic, compelling, gracious - the best, not the worst; the beautiful, not the ugly; things to praise, not things to curse. Put into practice what you learned from me, what you heard and saw and realized. Do that, and God, who makes everything work together, will work you into his most excellent harmonies. (The Message)

~

February 10 - Keep a Promise Today

Follow through today on a promise. As you do, watch Heaven open and blessings pour out.

2 Corinthians 1:20 - For all of God's promises find their "yes" of fulfillment in him. And as his "yes" and our "amen" ascend to God, we bring him glory. (TPT)

~

February 11 - The Lord Bless You and Keep You

Do not be offended today when someone misunderstands you. Instead, forgive. Be thankful for the good things, and remember who you are in God—His child, His friend, created for good. He is so proud of you.

Numbers 6:24-26: "The Lord bless you and keep you; the Lord make his face shine on you and be gracious to you; the Lord turn his face toward you and give you peace." (NIV)

~

February 12 - Watch for Answers to Prayer

Press into prayer ... and remember the prayers you used to pray that have not been answered yet. We were not created for unanswered prayer. Keep watching for the answers. Don't give up.

John 14:14 - You may ask me for anything in my name, and I will do it. (NIV)

~

February 13 - Miracle of Provision

Miracles are all around today. For you, it is a miracle of provision being poured out without you having to pay.

Psalm 145:16 - When You open up Your generous hand, it's full of blessings, Satisfying the longings of every living thing. (TPT)

~

February 14 - No Matter What!

If you have never read *The Shack* by Paul Young, read it. If you have read it, read it again. It is packed full of truth that sticks with you long after you have read it. God is a relational God. He is all about family—Father, Son, and Holy Spirit. He loves you no matter what; no matter how hard you may challenge Him. He is especially fond of you today, my friend.

"Don't ever discount the wonder of your tears. They can be healing waters and a stream of joy. Sometimes they are the best words the heart can speak." Wm. Paul Young – The Shack

Jeremiah 31:3 - "I have loved you with an everlasting love; I have drawn you with unfailing kindness." (NIV)

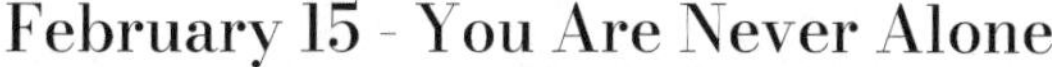

February 15 - You Are Never Alone

Sometimes we think we have to be tough to survive this life. We build walls and become hardened, afraid to show weakness for fear of failure or being hurt. But do you know God has our back? We are not alone. We can be who He made us to be. We can be vulnerable when we have the Creator of the Universe for a Papa. When we are brave enough to be who we are, trust is built in business and personal relationships. That's how we can change the world.

John 16:33 - "I have told you these things, so that in me you may have peace. In this world you will have trouble. But take heart! I have overcome the world." (NIV)

Hebrews 13:5 - "Never will I leave you; never will I forsake you." (NIV)

February 16 - Bless Your Helpers

There are those in your life that deserve honor for what they have done to give you a better chance in life. Bless them today.

Colossians 3:15 - Let the peace of Christ rule in your hearts, since as members of one body you were called to peace. And be thankful. (NIV)

February 17 - Brilliance for Something New

There is a bright clarity in the morning today to start a new project. Watch for a divine appointment.

2 Timothy 1:7 - For God has not given us a spirit of fear, but of power and of love and of a sound mind. (NKJV)

~

February 18 - The Wait Is Over

You have been in a period of transition where it seems what you hope for is just out of reach. That time is over. Step into your dream.

Habakkuk 2:3 - For still the vision awaits its appointed time; it hastens to the end—it will not lie. If it seems slow, wait for it; it will surely come; it will not delay. (ESV)

~

February 19 - Laugh

It's a good day to be silly. Lift up your head and see the joy before you. There is joy in Heaven, too. So we pray "on Earth as it is in Heaven."

Psalm 2:4 - The one enthroned in Heaven laughs. (NIV)

~

February 20 - It's a New Day

It's a new day—a clean canvas before you. What are you going to paint today? Let it be colorful and full of goodness.

Psalm 139:9 - If I fly with wings into the shining dawn, You're there! If I fly into the radiant sunset, You're there waiting! Wherever I go Your hand will guide me, Your strength will empower me. (TPT)

~

February 21 – Kickstart Your Day

Like coffee or tea is a good kickstart for your day, try a good Psalm or Proverb. Read a Psalm a day and read the Proverbs (thirty-one in all) that correspond with the day of the month. Listen ... God is speaking to you!

Proverbs 21:21 – Whoever pursues righteousness and love finds life, prosperity, and honor. (NIV)

~

February 22 - Those Clapping Trees

You will have peace today. If you can't find it, go back to where you lost it and regroup. Ask God to help you find your peace. Then take those steps forward into the light on the path He has set before you.

Isaiah 55:12 - You will go out in joy and be led forth in peace; the mountains and hills will burst into song before you, and all the trees of the field will clap their hands. (NIV)

~

February 23 Fresh Favor

God is giving you new tools to navigate your life.

Psalm 84:11 - For the Lord God is a sun and shield; the Lord bestows favor and honor; no good thing does he withhold from those whose walk is blameless. (NIV)

Psalm 90:17 - May the favor of the Lord our God rest on us; establish the work of our hands for us— yes, establish the work of our hands. (NIV)

~

February 24 Time to Receive

You have a role as guardian, protector, and provider—but know it is also okay to receive this from someone else. Open your heart. Don't be afraid to be vulnerable. There is great strength in vulnerability.

2 Corinthians 12:9 - And He said to me, "My grace is sufficient for you, for My strength is made perfect in weakness." (NKJV)

~

February 25 New Ideas Are Coming

Put your face in the sunshine today and just rest a few moments. Ideas are coming.

James 1:5 - If any of you lacks wisdom, let him ask God, who gives generously to all without reproach, and it will be given him. (ESV)

February 26 - Just Keep Learning

You are learning more about life and how interesting it is; like how sometimes the most beautiful things come in a not-so-beautiful package.

Proverbs 2:9-11 - Then you will understand what is right and just and fair - every good path, for wisdom will enter your heart, and knowledge will be pleasant to your soul. Discretion will protect you, and understanding will guard you. (NIV)

February 27 - Do What Brings You Strength

Do today what brings you strength—what makes you feel on top of things—what is exhilarating to you. For some it is a walk alone by a river. For others it is lunch with friends. You will be blessed beyond your wildest imagination.

Ephesians 6:10 - Be strong in the Lord and in the power of His might. (NIV)

February 28 - Just Play

Play today. Just play.

Psalm 45:7 - You are passionate for righteousness, and you hate lawlessness. This is why God, your God, crowns you with bliss above your fellow kings. He has anointed you, more than any other, with his oil of fervent joy, the very fragrance of heaven's gladness. (TPT)

~

Feb. 29 (Leap Year)

You've been graciously given an extra 1440 minutes this year (Leap Year) to listen for the still, sweet, voice of your Father. Take some time today. Ask Him a question. Then be quiet and listen for His response. May it be a sweet gift to you today.

James 1:17 – Every good and perfect gift is from above, coming down from the Father of the heavenly lights, who does not change like shifting shadows. (NIV)

March

March

March 1 - Tune In

Find times to tune out this month ... so you can tune in to the One who loves you more than anything.

Revelation 3:20 - Here I am! I stand at the door and knock. If anyone hears my voice and opens the door, I will come in and eat with that person, and they with me. (NIV)

March 2 - You Are an Encourager

Do you know you are making a difference? The words of your mouth, the way you live, and the way you love—they touch people more deeply than you know. God is sending you someone to encourage today.

1 Thessalonians 5:11 - Therefore encourage one another and build each other up, just as in fact you are doing. (NIV)

March 3 – Joy, Joy, Joy

There is a flow in the earth, a balance struck in nature that connects us with creation—that makes us revel in the beauty around us and the love we find in each other. This is a tangible picture of the love of God and His joy over what He has made. The joy we feel is His joy.

Psalm 16:11 - Now you've got my feet on the life path, all radiant from the shining of your face. Ever since you took my hand, I'm on the right way. (MSG)

March 4 – Happy Highs Coming

Like cold rain yields to sunshiny tomorrows, our lives can go from sadness and lows to happy highs. Always know that your day will get better, your life will be brighter. Declare it over your days and over your nights. Papa God's joy is to bless His kids. It is His kindness that leads us to change our ways and follow His love.

Psalm 149:9 – The Lord is good to all, and His tender mercies are over all His works. (NKJV)

Matthew 11:28-30 "Are you tired? Worn out? Burned out on religion? Come to me. Get away with me and you'll recover your life. I'll show you how to take a real rest. Walk with me and work with me—watch how I do it. Learn the unforced rhythms of grace. I won't lay anything heavy or ill-fitting on you. Keep company with me and you'll learn to live freely and lightly." (MSG)

~

March 5 - Who Are You?

Just as Band-Aids make our hurts better, so the promises of God can take a negative feeling about ourselves and turn it around to remembering who we are and who we belong to. We are not who our past says we are. We are who God says we are.

You are an adopted child of a good Father; brother and sister of His son, Jesus; heir of the abundance of Heaven; with a destiny to advance the Kingdom of God on Earth through His Holy Spirit. He calls you "friend."

Proverbs 3:5-6 – Trust in the Lord with all your heart and lean not on your own understanding. In all your ways, acknowledge Him, and He shall direct your paths. (NKJV)

~

March 6 - Ask God about Your Circumstances

If you are wondering why things aren't changing the way you would like them to ... or why a prayer has not been answered ... or why certain things are happening that don't seem to have answers— ask your Father in Heaven today. Then listen for His answers. Watch for His signs of promise. Hold fast to what He has promised in the past.

1 Thessalonians 5:18 - Give thanks in all circumstances; for this is God's will for you in Christ Jesus. (NIV)

~

March 7 - You Are God's Happy Thought

Do you ever wonder or worry about what others are thinking about you? Stop it! Start believing what God thinks about you. That is the truth ... always. Ask Him, then listen. He thinks you're the best!

"You are God's happy thought." - Leif Hetlund

Psalm 139:13 - For you created my inmost being; you knit me together in my mother's womb. (NIV)

Jeremiah 31:3 - "I have loved you with an everlasting love; I have drawn you with unfailing kindness." (NIV)

Zephaniah 3:17 - "The Lord your God is with you, the Mighty Warrior who saves. He will take great delight in you; in his love he will no longer rebuke you, but will rejoice over you with singing." (NIV)

~

March 8 - New Pathways

New pathways are unfolding. As you cast vision for your life, watch for those rolling green meadows of promise. Take the next steps and see how God blesses.

Revelation 21:5 - He who was seated on the throne said, "I am making everything new!" Then he said, "Write this down, for these words are trustworthy and true." (NIV)

~

March 9 - You Have All You Need

Longer days are dawning, and you will have lots of energy to accomplish what is in your heart to do. Divine health, healing, and abundant life are yours in this season.

Philippians 4:13 - I can do all things through Christ who strengthens me. (NKJV)

~

March 10 - Trust and Listen

Blessings are coming from some wild sources if you have the patience and awareness to trust and listen.

Luke 1:37 - For with God, nothing will be impossible. (NKJV)

~

March 11 - Move Ahead into Your Destiny

Passion is a tool you can use to know your calling, or what you were created to do. What are you passionate about? What do you love? What skills have you had the joy to develop? What do you dream of doing? Your passion can be as wonderful as drinking coffee with a special friend—or something as strategic as hoping to find the cure for cancer. Today you are moving ahead into your destiny.

"You see things; and you say, 'Why?' But I dream things that never were; and I say, 'Why not?'" – George Bernard Shaw

Ephesians 2:10 - We have become His poetry, a recreated people that will fulfill the destiny He has given each of us, for we are joined to Jesus, the Anointed One. Even before we were born, God planned in advance our destiny and the good works we would do to fulfill it. (TPT)

~

March 12 - The Spirit Is with You

Jesus always walked with the awareness of the Spirit of God upon Him. The Bible refers to the Holy Spirit as "like" a dove. How shall we walk as if the Spirit is with us? Gently, humbly, and always aware of the Presence. Be still.

John 16:13 - But when he, the Spirit of truth, comes, he will guide you into all the truth. He will not speak on his own; he will speak only what he hears, and he will tell you what is yet to come. (NIV)

Luke 4:18-19 - "The Spirit of the Lord is on me, because he has anointed me to proclaim good news to the poor. He has sent me to proclaim freedom for the prisoners and recovery of sight for the blind, to set the oppressed free, to proclaim the year of the Lord's favor." (NIV)

~

March 13 - Proud Papa

You may have had some hard things happen to you. You may think you have ruined any chance at a good life. You may even not like yourself much. But God sees it differently. You are a new creation. You are His child. You are His friend. He loves you and is proud of you.

1 John 1:3 - See what great love the Father has lavished on us, that we should be called children of God! (NIV)

Psalm 139:17-18 - Every single moment you are thinking of me! How precious and wonderful to consider, that You cherish me constantly in Your every thought! O God, Your desires toward me are more than the grains of sand on every shore! When I awake each morning, You're still thinking of me. (TPT)

~

March 14 - Be Free! Be Free!

What is truth? Truth is what God says about us and about a situation. The enemy of God—the devil—would like to keep us from that truth. He is a liar and a deceiver. How can we tell the difference? Well, if you are feeling bad about yourself, fearful, or prone to doing what you don't want to do, you are under the influence of a lie. Ask God for the truth. Declare His promises. Step into freedom today.

Galatians 5:1 - It is for freedom that Christ has set us free. (NIV)

Galatians 5:1 - Let me be clear, the Anointed One has set us free - not partially, but completely and wonderfully free! (TPT)

~

March 15 - A Day to Dance

It is a day to dance, to proclaim the joys of life with thankfulness and renewed hope. God is filling you with His joy today. Take and eat and dance!

2 Samuel 6 - Oh yes, I'll dance to God's glory—more recklessly even than this. And as far as I'm concerned . . . I'll gladly look like a fool.... (MSG)

Psalm 30: 11-12 - You did it: you changed wild lament into whirling dance.... (MSG)

~

March 16 - You Will Not Be Shaken

Though things around you may seem chaotic and jolting, you will not be shaken. You are able to stand firm.

Proverbs 18:10 - The name of the Lord is a fortified tower; the righteous run to it and are safe. (NIV)

Psalm 91:4 - His massive arms are wrapped around you, protecting you. You can run under His covering of majesty and hide. His faithfulness is a wrap-around shield keeping you from harm. (TPT)

~

March 17 - Hang on for the Wonderful

Hold on! What seems like a whirlwind today is propelling you into something new and wonderful.

"The future belongs to those who believe in the beauty of their dreams."

- Eleanor Roosevelt

Romans 15:13 - May the God of hope fill you with all joy and peace as you trust in him, so that you may overflow with hope by the power of the Holy Spirit. (NIV)

~

March 18 - Celebrate

It is a day for special celebration. What are you celebrating?

Psalm 149 - Hallelujah! Praise the Lord! It's time to sing to God a brand-new song, so that all His loving people will then hear how wonderful He is! May Israel be enthused with joy all because of Him, and may the sons of Zion pour out their joyful praises to their King! Break forth with dancing! Make music and sing God's praises with the rhythm of drums! For He enjoys His faithful lovers. He adorns the humble with His beauty, And He loves to give them the victory. (TPT)

~

March 19 - Let It Rain

Pouring rain refreshes the earth, and spiritual rain brings refreshment to the things of the spirit. You will see more clearly, know more surely, and discover more intimately the things of God today and in the days to come.

Hebrews 6:7 - Land that drinks in the rain often falling on it and that produces a crop useful to those for who it is farmed receives the blessing of God. (NIV)

1 Kings 18:41 - Elijah said to Ahab, "upon your feet! Eat and drink - celebrate! Rain is on the way; I hear it coming." (MSG)

~

March 20 - You Are His Favorite

To Papa God, you are His favorite child. Stop thinking you are less than, or that you are unworthy. You are worthy because you are His. Crawl up into His lap and let Him hold you today.

Ephesians 1:5 - For it was always in His perfect plan to adopt us as His delightful children, so that His tremendous grace that cascades over us would bring Him glory - for the same love He has for His Beloved One, Jesus, He has for us! And this unfolding plan brings Him great pleasure. (TPT)

~

March 21 - Listen

Take your shoes off. Touch the ground. Feel the sun on your face. Listen to a bird sing. Connect with nature today, and you will hear God's voice. What is He saying?

"I love to think of nature as an unlimited broadcasting station, through which God speaks to us every hour, if we will only tune in." George Washington Carver

~

March 22 - Created to Be Creative

Try this. Buy some children's watercolors at the store. Take a sheet of copy paper. Close your eyes. Ask God to give you a picture. What do you see? Paint that. It doesn't have to be a Monet. It can just be a swirl of color. You are designed in the image of the Creator of the Universe. Creativity was put into your DNA. A simple creative act will unlock more of who you were created to be and what you were created to do. Be a child. Have fun.

Genesis 1:27 - So God created mankind in his own image... (NIV)

~

March 23 - Prosperity and Abundance

Today is a prosperous day. Abundance is coming—not only in your finances, but in your soul, your health, in relationships, and in joy.

Philippians 4:19 - And my God will meet all your needs according to the riches of his glory in Christ Jesus. (NIV)

~

March 24 - A Better Reality

There is a realm of reality that is more real than what you see. God is going to introduce you to more of that reality in the next few months. It is a realm of beauty with angelic activity, and will reveal more of why you were created and what you really have in your heart to do and be.

1 Corinthians 13:12 - We don't yet see things clearly. We're squinting in a fog, peering through a mist. But it won't be long before the weather clears and the sun shines bright! We'll see it all then, see it all as clearly as God sees us, knowing him directly just as he knows us! (MSG)

~

March 25 Watch for a Divine Appointment

A divine appointment will bring a surprise, as well as new ideas and strategies this week.

Philippians 2:13 - God will continually revitalize you, implanting within you the passion to accomplish the good things you desire to do. (TPT)

~

March 26 You Are So Special to God

You are so special to your Father in Heaven. Do you really know that? He is revealing more of His heart to you today and in the days to come. Be intentional in your awareness of Him throughout your days.

John 17:23 - "For they will see that You love each one of them with the same passionate love that You have for Me." (Jesus praying to His Father for you and for me.) *(TPT)*

~

March 27 - God's Talking

God is always talking to us. He speaks in different ways—through friends, the Bible, a picture, a still small voice, an audible voice, coincidences, or a sense about something. He uses our imagination that He gave us to communicate, too. He will show you more in days to come how He speaks to you.

Isaiah 30:21 - Whether you turn to the right or to the left, your ears will hear a voice behind you, saying, "This is the way; walk in it." (NIV)

~

March 28 - As Close as Your Breath

Does it ever seem like God is out of reach? God wants you to know He is as close as your breath.

Albert Einstein said, “There are only two ways to live your life. One is as though nothing is a miracle. The other is as if everything is.”

James 4:8 - Draw near to God and He will draw near to you. (NKJV)

~

March 29 - Today - A New Call to Love

To serve the Lord does not mean we are slaves. He calls us friend. He only asks us to do what brings us great joy already—what we know in our hearts we were created for. Few are called into church ministry. What we are really called to is to love—each other, friends, neighbors, the hopeless, and the nations. Serve the Lord by finding a new way to reach out and share His love today.

1 Corinthians 13:13 - And now abide faith, hope, love, these three; but the greatest of these is love. (NKJV)

~

March 30 - Through a Child's Eyes

When I was little, I used to close my eyes tight and see beautiful tapestries and carpets. Were they the carpets in the heavenly mansion? I don't know. But today you will see through a child's eyes the beauty of Creation. Breathe deep.

Psalm 119:18 – Be generous with me and I'll live a full life; not for a minute will I take my eyes off your road. Open my eyes so I can see what you show me of your miracle-wonders. (MSG)

~

March 31 - You're Getting Stronger

Today is a day of breakthrough into the deeper things of God. Your life is being enriched and fortified.

Philippians 4:13 - Whatever I have, wherever I am, I can make it through anything in the One who makes me who I am. (MSG)

Philippians 4:13 - I can do all things through Christ who strengthens me. (NKJV)

April

April

April 1 - It's a Healing Day

Step into new health today. There is an anointing for healing.

Acts 19:11-12 - God did powerful things through Paul, things quite out of the ordinary. The word got around, and people started taking pieces of clothing - handkerchiefs and scarves and the like - that had touched Paul's skin and then touching the sick with them. The touch did it - they were healed and whole. (MSG)

(Just as the story about Paul above, I pray today that as you see and read this post written especially for you, that you, too, are healed in whatever way you need it.)

~

April 2 - Live Fully Confident

There are walls that stand between us and God sometimes—walls of past hurts, walls of self-preservation, and walls of isolation from anything that might hurt us again. God is lovingly taking walls down in your life. He wants you to live fully confident of His love and protection.

Psalm 23:1-3 - God is my Fierce Protector and my Provider; I always have more than enough. Like a Shepherd He finds a resting place for me in His luxury-love. His tracks take me to the quiet brooks of bliss, an oasis of grace. That's where He restores and revives my life. (TPT)

~

April 3 - Hope Realized

Sometimes we replay the videos of our past over and over in our heads. Some of those videos keep us stuck and regretful and sick. Today, God wants to take those from us and give us new videos of future hope and destiny. He wants us to be free.

Proverbs 13:12 - Hope deferred makes the heart sick, but a dream fulfilled is a tree of life. (NLT)

Philippians 3:13-15 - Brethren, I do not count myself to have apprehended; but one thing I do, forgetting those things which are behind and reaching forward to those things which are ahead, I press toward the goal for the prize of the upward call of God in Christ Jesus. (NKJV)

Galatians 5:1 - It is for freedom that Christ has set us free. (NIV)

April 4 - Heaven's Text Message

Close your eyes and imagine a phone call or text from Heaven. Make it joyful. God is a happy God. Happy is what He wants for you, too. What will you talk about? What questions will you ask Him? What questions will He ask you? What do you long to tell Him?

John 1:5 - And this Living Expression is the Light that bursts through gloom. (TPT)

April 5 - A New Thought Is Coming

We need to change the way we think—instead of worry, trust; instead of fear, hope; instead of sickness, health; instead of anxiety, peace; instead of doom, crazy abundance. You get the picture. There is power in our thoughts and words to change the reality of our lives. Instead of negative thoughts and worries, declare aloud daily the promises of God and see circumstances change.

Job 22:28 - You will also declare a thing, and it will be established for you; So light will shine on your ways. (NKJV)

April 6 - Encouragement from You

Someone in your world needs your word of encouragement today. Look around. See that shy teenager? What about your widowed neighbor? How could you encourage a family member online? One word from you will make all the difference in their day.

Proverbs 16:24 - Pleasant words are like a honeycomb, sweetness to the soul and health to the bones. (NKJV)

~

April 7 - Simple Belief

Jesus calls us to simply believe. If you never learned anything else about the doctrine of the church, you could trust that this would be enough. Believe in the One sent by God to a hopeless world to bring hope, renewal, restoration, and relationship with the Father. Do you believe? Tell Him now.

Acts 16:29-31 - The jailer called for a light. When he saw that they were still in their cells, he rushed in and fell trembling at their feet. Then he led Paul and Silas outside and asked, "What must I do to be saved?" They answered, "Believe in the Lord Jesus and you will be saved – you and all your family." (TPT)

~

April 8 - If You Shine, They Will Come

Every person carries an aspect of the nature of God that no one else carries. You are so important to everyone around you because of that. We are not meant to be alone in the world when we have such an awesome Papa's nature.

Matthew 5:14 - You are the light of the world. A town built on a hill cannot be hidden. (NIV)

April 9 - Your Father's Child

You may be older, but you are still a child to your Father in Heaven. That childlikeness—that spirit of joy, trust, innocence, and love—are a blessing to your Papa and to your family and friends.

Matthew 18:4 - Whoever continually humbles himself to become like this little child is the greatest one in heaven's kingdom realm. (TPT)

April 10 - The Game Changer

Love makes all the difference. That's all He wants you to know today.

1 John 4:11 - Beloved, if God so loved us, we also ought to love one another. (NKJV)

April 11 - Receive Your Gift

So much is being birthed in springtime. Something new is arising in you, too. You sense it and feel it. Let it come and consider it a gift to you—and also to others.

Psalm 84:11 - For the Lord God is brighter than the brilliance of sunrise! Wrapping Himself around me like a shield, He is so generous with His gifts of grace and glory! (TPT)

~

April 12 - Permission to Fly

Have you ever dreamed you can fly? I have. I actually know how to take off, fly, and land in my dreams. God wants you to fly with Him—to know you aren't stuck—you aren't a victim—rather you are free to be and to explore, to hope and to dream. Fly with Him!

Galatians 5:1 - Let me be clear, the Anointed One has set us free - not partially, but completely and wonderfully free! (TPT)

~

April 13 - Fresh Air

There is a freshness you can feel with God that is like a crisp spring morning in the mountains. Today, spend time with your Creator and breathe Him in. It can be through prayer, or just being still and listening.

Romans 15:13 - Oh! May the God of green hope fill you up with joy, fill you up with peace, so that your believing lives, filled with the life-giving energy of the Holy Spirit, will brim over with hope! (MSG)

~

April 14 - Good, Good Life Plans

Do you know God sees the end from the beginning in our lives? Know that He already has your back, and the results are going to be wonderful.

Isaiah 46:10 - I make known the end from the beginning, from ancient times, what is still to come. I say, "My purpose will stand, and I will do all that I please." (NIV)

1 Corinthians 2:9 - "Eye has not seen, nor ear heard, nor have entered into the heart of man the things which God has prepared for those who love Him." (NKJV)

~

April 15 – Miraculous Provision

Do you have debts? Do you know when Jesus and His disciples needed to pay taxes that Jesus just summoned a fish which delivered the money for the tax? Pray, and trust Him for wisdom and provision over finances. Lord, let my friends see Your miracles of provision.

Prayer of Jabez:

1 Chronicles 4:10 - And Jabez called on the God of Israel saying, "Oh, that You would bless me indeed, and enlarge my territory, that Your hand would be with me, and that You would keep me from evil, that I may not cause pain!" So God granted him what he requested. (NKJV)

~

April 16 - Expect a Turnaround

The day our Lord died on the cross, there was great devastation in the land. But on the third day, the story changed forever. This could be a picture of something in your life that seems hopeless. Expect a complete turnaround.

Acts 13:29-30 - When they had carried out all that was written about him, they took him down from the cross and laid him in a tomb. But God raised him from the dead. (NIV)

~

April 17 - Thirty Days...

Creativity is in the air. You are made in the image of a wonderful Creator who created not only the world and universe, but your own imagination. What is He showing you about your destiny ... your passion ... your purpose? Write it down and pray over it. See what happens in the next thirty days.

Ephesians 3:20 - Never doubt God's mighty power to work in you and accomplish all this. He will achieve infinitely more than your greatest request, your most unbelievable dream, and exceed your wildest imagination! He will outdo them all, for His miraculous power constantly energizes you! (TPT)

~

April 18 - It's a Birthday for Something New

God is giving birth to something new in your heart and spirit. As you pay attention to this, begin to declare its reality in your life today and watch it begin to emerge with joy over your future.

"It's been said that every little stream is born secretly believing it's a river, until it becomes one." Ray Hughes

Isaiah 43:19 - See, I am doing a new thing! Now it springs up; do you not perceive it? I am making a way in the wilderness and streams in the wasteland. (NIV)

Revelation 21:5 - Then He who sat on the throne said, "Behold, I make all things new." And He said to me "Write, for these words are true and faithful." (NKJV)

~

April 19 - He's a Good, Good, God

There is something special about your day today— a new idea, a new toy, a new relationship, or a travel plan. God is going to use this special day to remind you of His goodness.

Psalm 27:13 - I remain confident of this: I will see the goodness of the Lord in the land of the living. (NIV)

~

April 20 - Dreams Are Increasing

Night dreams are increasing. God speaks to us in our dreams. Write them down and ask Him for the meaning.

Acts 2:17 - In the last days, God says, I will pour out my Spirit on all people. Your sons and daughters will prophesy, your young men will see visions, your old men will dream dreams. (NIV)

~

April 21 Abuzz with Life

The air is abuzz with life and newness—a sweet picture of promise and better days. Breathe it in today, and you will sense how much you are loved by your Father God.

Psalm 97:11 - For He sows seeds of light within His lovers, releasing a harvest in the souls of the righteous; seeds of joy burst forth for the lovers of God. (TPT)

~

April 22 Good Day

Blessings are coming from someone close to you.

Romans 12:10 - Be devoted to one another in love. Honor one another above yourselves. (NIV)

Genesis 12 - I'll bless those who bless you." (The Message)

~

April 23 Your Living Hope

Just as butterflies are emerging from their cocoons, floating on the breeze in a display of nature's beauty, you are discovering your own wings. The winter is over. Spring is here. Be free and fly.

Proverbs 23:18 - Your future is bright and filled with a living hope that will never fade away. (TPT)

~

April 24 - Sheer Delight

Today is a day of bright color—a day that makes you want to dance and shout. So, do it!

2 Samuel 6 - David, ceremonially dressed in priest's linen, danced with great abandon before God. (MSG)

Psalm 65:12-13 - Luxuriant green pastures boast of Your bounty as you make every hillside blossom with joy. The grazing meadows are covered with flocks and the fertile valleys are clothed with grain, each one dancing and shouting for joy, creation's celebration! And they're all singing their songs of praise to You! (TPT)

~

April 25 - Refreshing Rain

Spring showers are not sad. They are life-giving and come with a sweetness and fragrance of cleansing and awakening. God is refreshing your spirit like that.

Hosea 6:3 - As sure as dawn breaks, so sure is his daily arrival. He comes as rain comes, as spring rain refreshing the ground. (MSG)

~

April 26 An Everlasting Love

The sweet fragrance of blooming sage in a mountain rain is like the fragrance of love that encompasses your life today. Know you are loved with an everlasting love.

Jeremiah 31:3 - God told them, "I've never quit loving you and never will. Expect love, love, and more love! (MSG)

~

April 27 It's a Good Day for a Miracle

Today, step into your healing. God is powerfully present to heal you—physically and inside, too. Ask him. Find someone to pray with you in the name of Jesus the Healer.

Luke 5:12 - 13: While Jesus was in one of the towns, a man came along who was covered with leprosy. When he saw Jesus, he fell with his face to the ground and begged him, "Lord, if you are willing, you can make me clean." Jesus reached out his hand and touched the man. "I am willing," he said. "Be clean!" And immediately the leprosy left him. (NIV)

My prayer for you, my reader: Be healed in Jesus' Name. Amen!

~

April 28 What Is Your Destiny?

You have a divine destiny. Today you will discover more about what that means. It has to do with what you love and what is already "in your hand." It holds creative gifting and God's entrusted call on your life. What an exciting journey you are on with Him.

Philippians 3:12 - I admit that I haven't yet acquired the absolute fullness that I'm pursuing, but I run with passion into His abundance so that I may reach the purpose that Jesus Christ has called me to fulfill and wants me to discover. (TPT)

Habakkuk 2:3 - For still the vision awaits its appointed time; it hastens to the end--it will not lie. If it seems slow, wait for it; it will surely come; it will not delay. (ESV)

~

April 29 - What Life Do You Want to Live?

You may think there is nothing you can do about the problems and situations in your life, but God says there is all hope to bring you blessing upon blessing. We start with changing the way we think—then our reality follows suit. Try it! Declare the life you want to live!

Job 22:28 - You will also declare a thing, and it will be established for you; so light will shine on your ways. (NKJV)

~

April 30 – A Personal God

Today you will learn a new side of God you didn't know, for He is personal and relational. He is close, and He wants to keep you close.

Psalm 46:1 - God, You're such a safe and strong place to hide! You're a tested help in time of trouble. More than enough and always available whenever I need You. (TPT)

May

May

May 1 - Assurance for Today

God wants you to know today that ... "it is going to be okay."

Hebrews 11:1 - Now faith is confidence in what we hope for and assurance about what we do not see. (NIV)

~

May 2 - Happy Raindrops

Raindrops keep falling on your head and in your heart. Happy raindrops. Let them create an atmosphere around you that carries the fragrance of fresh mowed grass, roses, pine trees, and horses.

Psalm 104:13 - From Your kindness you send the rain to water the mountains from the upper rooms of your palace. Your goodness brings forth fruit for all to enjoy. (TPT)

~

May 3 - Nature and Nature

Some leaves are shaped to curl upward. Some are weeping. Some are quaking. Some offer protection and shade. Others are prickly and sharp. If you were a tree, what would your leaves be like? I think mine would be golden aspen leaves, quaking in the brilliant sunshine.

Psalm 104:24 - O Lord, what an amazing variety of all you have created! Wild and wonderful is this world you have made, while wisdom was there at your side. (TPT)

~

May 4 - Remembering Our Dreams

When playing, children imagine themselves in different roles—as princesses, firemen, tractor drivers, or cowboys and cowgirls, to name a few. Do you remember what you believed you were when you were little? It quite likely has something to do with your destiny now.

Proverbs 19:21 - We humans keep brainstorming options and plans, but God's purpose prevails. (MSG)

~

May 5 - A Colorful Feast

Take a moment to slow down and appreciate a piece of art or poetry today. How does it speak to you? Know that in the same way it speaks to you God can also speak to you. His Word is full of color, art, and poetry—a feast for the hungry.

John 1:1 - In the beginning was the Word, and the Word was with God, and the Word was God. He was in the beginning with God. (NKJV)

John 1:1-9 - In the very beginning God was already there. And before His Face was His Living Expression. And this Living Expression was with God, yet fully God! They were together - face to face in the very beginning! And through His creative inspiration this Living Expression made all things, for nothing has existence apart from Him! Life came into being because of Him, For His Life is light for all humanity. And this Living Expression Is the Light that bursts through all gloom. The Light that darkness could not diminish! (TPT)

~

May 6 - Live in Hope ... Be a Light

Always remember that out of the darkest clouds, a rainbow can break through. Out of the blackest night, the Milky Way bursts across the sky. Sunrises are more spectacular when there are clouds in the sky. Joy is more joyful when the heart has also known sadness. It's life. It's your life. You can choose to live in the light and be a light.

Matthew 5:14 - Here's another way to put it: You're here to be light, bringing out the God-colors in the world. God is not a secret to be kept. We're going public with this, as public as a city on a hill. If I make you light-bearers, you don't think I'm going to hide you under a bucket, do you? I'm putting you on a light stand. Now that I've put you there on a hilltop, on a light stand—shine! Keep open house; be generous with your lives.

By opening up to others, you'll prompt people to open up with God, this generous Father in heaven. (MSG)

~

May 7 - A Super Partner

Often, we speak of striving to be something or to do something. Striving is not from God. It is all under our own power. God's invitation is to partner with Him in every circumstance. He loves us right where we are, then helps us get to an amazing purpose He has for us.

Psalm 124:8 - God's strong name is our help, the same God who made heaven and earth. (MSG)

~

May 8 - The Power of Good Thinking

Call it what you will: The power of positivity, looking on the bright side, being an optimist or a dreamer, or putting mind over matter. It is true that setting our minds on promises and dreams has power to overcome negative activity coming against our lives.

Romans 12:2 – Stop imitating the ideals and opinions of the culture around you, but be inwardly transformed by the Holy Spirit through a total reformation of how you think. This will empower you to discern God's will as you live a beautiful life, satisfying and perfect in his eyes. (TPT)

~

May 9 - The Creator of the Clouds

When I was young, my friend and I would lie in the grass facing up, quite convinced we could make clouds dissipate with our minds. Oh, if we could only have set our minds on the One who actually designed those clouds—getting to know Him in a practical, personal way.

Psalm 104:3 - He makes the clouds his chariot and rides on the wings of the wind. (NIV)

~

May 10 - He Fashioned You

Just as each rose has its own delicate fragrance, or each voice has its own stamp, or each human being has his own unique DNA, you are intentionally designed by Papa God.

Psalm 139:13-14,16 - You formed my innermost being, shaping my delicate inside and my intricate outside, and wove them all together in my mother's womb. I thank you God, for making me so mysteriously complex! Everything you do is marvelously breathtaking! It simply amazes me to think about it! How thoroughly you know me, Lord! ...You saw who You created me to be, before I came to be! (TPT)

~

May 11 - Trust in God Your Healer

Do you need physical healing? Today is a good day to take the next steps toward that. Ask God for wisdom. If needed, call your doctor. Then, trust in God your Healer.

Exodus 15:26 - "For I am the Lord who heals you." (NIV)

Psalm 103:1-6 - Bless the Lord, O my soul; and all that is within me, bless His holy name! Bless the Lord, O my soul, and forget not all His benefits: Who forgives all your iniquities, Who heals all your diseases, Who redeems your life from destruction, Who crowns you with lovingkindness and tender mercies, Who satisfies your mouth with good things, so that your youth is renewed like the eagle's. (NKJV)

~

May 12 - Amazing You

If you ever stopped to think about how awesome you are, you would be in awe—complex, intelligent, problem solver, overcomer, able to create, invent, procreate, and learn—with a body that responds to injury by healing, that can feel compassion and love, joy and hope. That is YOU.

Genesis 1:27 - So God created mankind in his own image, in the image of God he created them; male and female he created them. (NIV)

Genesis 1:31 - God looked over everything he had made; it was so good, so very good! (MSG)

~

May 13 - Faith Releases Rewards

If you love God and seek to know Him more, you have a promise of His rewards over your life.

Hebrews 11:6 - And without faith it is impossible to please God, because anyone who comes to him must believe that he exists and that he rewards those who earnestly seek him. (NIV)

John 15:7 - "If you abide in Me, and My words abide in you, you will ask what you desire, and it shall be done for you." (NKJV)

~

May 14 - You Deserve a Rest

Today is a day of completion. You have worked hard and learned much. Now, just like God rested after creating the world, you are to rest.

Genesis 2:2 - By the seventh day God had finished the work he had been doing; so on the seventh day he rested from all his work. (NIV)

Psalm 116:7 - Return to your rest, my soul, for the Lord has been good to you. (NIV)

~

May 15 - Dream Talks

When all is quiet and our minds are at rest in sleep, God sometimes speaks to us. Sometimes He'll wake us. Other times He will speak through dreams. Pay attention to thoughts that come in the night. Declare God's protection over your sleep and dreams.

Genesis 31:11 - The angel of God said to me in the dream, "Jacob." I answered, "Here I am." (NIV)

Matthew 2:13 – Now when they had departed, behold, an angel of the Lord appeared to Joseph in a dream... (ESV)

~

May 16 - Say "Hi" to Your Angels

Movies depict angels as watching over us from clouds and buildings. But do you know angelic activity is all around you? You have angels. Your children have angels. They are sent to us by God for protection and service to us.

Hebrews 1:14 - Are not all angels ministering spirits sent to serve those who will inherit salvation? (NIV)

~

May 17 - You Shall Hear God's Voice

The sound of a brook, the chirp of a squirrel, the song of an early morning bird, and the coolness of a breeze—they all fill us up, waking our senses. God's voice is like that. Today, tomorrow, and in days to come, listen for it.

Psalm 143:7-10 If you wake me each morning with the sound of your loving voice, I'll go to sleep each night trusting in you. (MSG)

~

May 18 - Hone Your Senses

Where do you live? The country? The city? A senior home? A college? A small town? No matter where you are, you can find beauty all around you. Your senses are getting sharper in this season. You will become aware of something new and beautiful.

Psalm 121:1 – I lift up my eyes to the mountains - where does my help come from? My help comes from the Lord, the maker of heaven and earth. (NIV)

~

May 19 - You Are Thought About

Someone close to you is thinking of you today. Give them a call or send a note. It will bless them more than you can imagine.

John 15:12-13 - Love each other as I have loved you. Greater love has no one than this; to lay down one's life for one's friends. (NIV)

~

May 20 - You Are Blessed and So Are They

Oh, you are so tough. So strong. So independent. But wait. We all need each other. Don't be afraid to ask for help today. Not only do you need it, but someone needs to feel the blessing of being asked.

Philippians 2:4 - Let each of you look out not only for his own interests, but also for the interests of others. (NKJV)

Luke 6:38 - Give, and it will be given to you. A good measure, pressed down, shaken together and running over, will be poured into your lap. For with the measure you use, it will be measured to you. (NIV)

Proverbs 15:33 - The fear of the Lord is the instruction of wisdom, and before honor is humility. (NKJV)

~

May 21 - Desire Fulfilled

Something you have desired for a long time is finally coming true for you. Are you ready?

Proverbs 13:12 - Hope deferred makes the heart sick; but a longing fulfilled is a tree of life. (NIV)

~

May 22 - Never Give Up Hope

If something is trying to bring you down, don't let it. Say no! Faith is hope in what isn't seen. Trust in the One who is able. There is all hope.

Hebrews 11:1 - Now faith is the substance of things hoped for, the evidence of things not seen. (NKJV)

Romans 15:13 - May the God of hope fill you with all joy and peace as you trust in him, so that you may overflow with hope by the power of the Holy Spirit. (NIV)

~

May 23 - Where Is Your Peace?

Let peace be your guide today. A decision needs to be made. God's peace is a tool to know which way to go.

Colossians 3:15-16 - Let the peace of Christ rule in your hearts, since as members of one body you were called to peace. And be thankful. (NIV)

~

May 24 - There Is Help to Move Forward

The presence of God is kind of like the wind. We can't see it, but we know it's there. Open your spiritual eyes and look into His eyes. Let Him help you move forward.

Isaiah 41:13 - For I am the Lord your God who takes hold of your right hand and says to you, do not fear; I will help you. (NIV)

John 9:37 – Jesus replied, "You're looking right at him. He's speaking with you. It's me, the one in front of you now." (TPT) (Jesus was speaking to the man He healed of blindness. Even now, He is saying this to us. "It's me, the one in front of you now.")

~

May 25 - Revel

God takes great pleasure in all He created for us. We should take pleasure in it, too. Oh, I love my coffee beans today. I love the trees and flowers. I love my family. I love writing. What do you love today?

Psalm 104:31 - The glory of God—let it last forever! Let God enjoy his creation! (MSG)

Genesis 1:31 - God looked over everything he had made; it was so good, so very good! (MSG)

May 26 Fan the Ember!

Something you have worked for, hoped for, seems to be almost dead. But there is an ember. Fan it into flame and watch it spring to life.

2 Timothy 1:6 - For this reason I remind you to fan into flame the gift of God, which is in you through the laying on of my hands. (NLV)

Habakkuk 2:2-3 - "Write this. Write what you see. Write it out in big block letters so that it can be read on the run. This vision-message is a witness pointing to what's coming. It aches for the coming–it can hardly wait! And it doesn't lie. If it seems slow in coming, wait. It's on its way. It will come right on time. (MSG)

May 27 - Who Needs You?

No matter if you are an extrovert or introvert, we all need people. We all need peace and quiet; we all need alone times; and we all need celebration times with others. Your spirit is so attractive to others. Your kindness invites friendship. Your joy is infectious. Someone needs you today. Don't hide.

Proverbs 27:9 - Sweet friendships refresh the soul, and awaken our hearts with joy, for good friends are like the anointing oil that yields the fragrant incense of God's presence. (TPT)

May 28 - Slay That Giant

Today is an overcoming day. It's a day for healing, a day for meeting that thing that has challenged you for too long. Meet it head on and enter into a new season of freedom. You can do it.

1 Samuel 17:26 - "Who is this uncircumcised Philistine, that he should defy the armies of the living God?" (NIV)

Isaiah 54:17 - "No weapon formed against you shall prosper, and every tongue which rises against you in judgment You shall condemn. This is the heritage of the servants of the Lord, and their righteousness is from Me," says the Lord. (NIV)

Psalm 91:11 - For He will command His angels concerning you to guard you in all your ways. (NIV)

~

May 29 - Chase Brilliance

If you have been thinking of taking a class, learning a new skill, or going back to school, today is a great day to take a step.

Proverbs 1:5 - Let the wise hear and increase in learning, and the one who understands obtain guidance. (ESV)

Romans 12:2 - Be transformed by the renewing of your mind. (Paraphrase from NIV)

~

May 30 - You Have Influence

We all have a realm of influence—at work, at school, or at home. Today you will release joy and light into that realm, and people will notice it.

Matthew 5:16 - In the same way, let your light shine before others, that they may see your good deeds and glorify your Father in heaven. (NIV)

~

May 31 - Green Day

Green is a color of prosperity, new beginnings, life, and abundance. Today is a green day for you. Breathe it in and expect some blessings.

Revelations 21:5 - "I am making everything new." (NIV)

June

June

June 1 - The Good Invader

Worry, despair, complaining, doubting, fear, and other negative things are NOT of God. If you find yourself doing any of these, recognize it and repent. Repent simply means to change the way you think. Have another thought. Believe in the ability of the Creator of the Universe to invade your situations with His goodness.

Psalm 94:17-19 - Unless the Lord had given me help, I would soon have dwelt in the silence of death. When I said, "My foot is slipping, your unfailing love, O Lord, supported me. When anxiety was great within me, your consolation brought joy to my soul." (NIV)

Psalm 91:14-15 - "Because he loves me," says the Lord, "I will rescue him; I will protect him, for he acknowledges my name. He will call upon me, and I will answer him; I will be with him in trouble...." (NIV)

~

June 2 - Sweet Dreams

Before you go to sleep tonight, declare you are going to sleep well, dream big, and wake refreshed. Key things are happening for you as you slumber.

Psalm 4:8 - In peace I will lie down and sleep, for you alone, Lord, make me dwell in safety. (NIV)

~

June 3 - Star-Like

You can look at the night sky and know the stars you see are also on display for others on the other side of the world. Yet they are such a gift to you. That's how God is. Personal. Just for you, yet available to all. What a Papa.

Jeremiah 31:3 - The Lord appeared to us in the past, saying: "I have loved you with an everlasting love. I have drawn you with unfailing kindness." (NIV)

~

June 4 - You Are His Favorite

John the disciple called himself the one Jesus loved. We know Jesus loves us all, but we can also feel like His favorite because of how He favors us. Today He wants to show you that you are His favorite.

Psalm 84:11 - For the Lord God is a sun and shield; the Lord bestows favor and honor; no good thing does he withhold from those whose walk is blameless. (NIV)

June 5 - Awe-Inspiring

Just as Jesus came as Son of Man to point the way to the Father in Heaven, there are signs every day that point us in the direction of our Papa. The amazing Creation is one of those signs. Oh, how He loves us that He would make us something just so we can experience awe.

Romans 1:20 - For since the creation of the world God's invisible qualities—his eternal power and divine nature—have been clearly seen, being understood from what has been made, so that people are without excuse. (NIV)

Revelation 4:11 - "You are worthy, O Lord, to receive glory and honor and power; for you created all things, and by Your will they exist and were created." (NIV)

June 6 - You Are a Breath of Fresh Air

From God's perspective, our lives are but a breath on this Earth. Will your life be the fresh, deep breath that brings life to you and others?

Isaiah 55:12 - "You will go out in joy and be led forth in peace; the mountains and hills will burst into song before you, and all the trees of the field will clap their hands." (NIV)

June 7 - Another Step into Heaven ... on Earth

One of the names of God is Ancient of Days. He is present today, will be present in the future, and has always been present since time began. He is unchanging in character, loves us completely, and is our link to eternity. Today, the Ancient of Days is taking you a step further into this realm that is Heaven on Earth.

Matthew 6:10 - Your kingdom come. Your will be done. On earth as it is in heaven. (NKJV)

~

June 8 - Bring Peace, Joy, and Hope

Did you know you bring the Lord's presence wherever you go? If you are a friend of God, He goes with you—He in you. You in Him—both changing the world around you. So, get 'er done! You will bring peace, joy, and hope today into someone's atmosphere.

1 John 4:7 – Beloved, let us love one another, for love is of God, and everyone who loves is born of God and knows God. (NKJV)

~

June 9 - Something's Brewing

Can you feel it? Something is brewing ... being prepared ... about to be released. Position yourself to receive what God is about to give you.

Psalm 138:8 - You keep every promise you've ever made to me! Since Your love for me is constant and endless, I ask You Lord, to finish every good thing that you've begun in me! (TPT)

~

June 10 - Breakthrough

You have been pushing against a wall of resistance for some time. Today that wall is beginning to crumble. Breakthrough is about to happen in your situation.

2 Samuel 5:20 – So David went to Baal Perazim, and David defeated them there; and he said, "The Lord has broken out against my enemies before me." (NKJV)

Breakthrough: Any significant or sudden advance, development, achievement, or increase, as in scientific knowledge or diplomacy, that removes a barrier to progress. (Dictionary.com)

~

June 11 - Blessed Hands

God gave us hands to help ourselves. We eat with them, help others with them, and work with them. They are such a gift to us and others. Today God is establishing something new for your hands.

Psalm 90:17 - May the favor of the Lord our God rest on us; establish the work of our hands for us - yes, establish the work of our hands.

~

June 12 - Sweet Solitude

No matter where we live on Earth—or how crowded or noisy or silent or isolated—there is a place we can go to be with God that is comforting, restful, full of life, and surrounded by beauty. The eyes of your heart are more aware today.

Mark 1:35 – The next morning, Jesus got up long before daylight, left the house while it was dark, and made his way to a secluded place to give himself to prayer." (TPT)

Psalm 46:10 - "Be still and know that I am God...." (NIV)

~

June 13 - Godly Possible

If God sees the end from the beginning, He already knows how your situation will turn out. It will turn out the best way possible—not humanly possible, but Godly possible.

Isaiah 46:10 - I make known the end from the beginning, from ancient times, what is still to come. I say, "My purpose will stand, and I will do all that I please." (NIV)

Matthew 19:26 - Jesus looked at them and said, "With man this is impossible, but with God all things are possible." (NIV)

Ephesians 3:20 - He will achieve infinitely more than your greatest request, your most unbelievable dream, and exceed your wildest imagination! He will outdo them all, for His miraculous power constantly energizes you! (TPT)

~

June 14 - A Promise in Process

Look back on your life. What dreams have you fulfilled? What prayers have been answered? What gave you the most joy? That is what is in process now for all that has not been answered yet. God makes promises and He keeps them.

John. 7:37 - On the last day, that great day of the feast, Jesus stood and cried out, saying, "If anyone thirsts, let him come to Me and drink. (NKJV)

~

June 15 - Look for the Good Part

Creation is so intricate and has such wisdom. The marigold is designed to not only be strikingly beautiful, but to protect a vegetable garden from aphids. The cactus not only provides food, but delights the heart when it bursts into its surprising blooms. A two-year-old child can bring both the greatest of frustration and the happiest of pleasure. There is more happening in your situation than you are seeing right now. Look for the good part.

Philippians 4:8 - I'd say you'll do best by filling your minds and meditating on things true, noble, reputable, authentic, compelling, gracious—the best, not the worst; the beautiful, not the ugly; things to praise, not things to curse. (MSG)

~

June 16 - Got Wisdom?

Wisdom designed ways to keep the squirrels in my yard from devouring the food meant for birds. Some of the biggest problems are solved not through destroying the source (the squirrel), but outsmarting it. Joy, cleverness, and thinking outside the box are fun ways to overcome issues with work, relationships, and even health. Where does that wisdom come from? The Holy Spirit —who is with us all the time—given to us by our Loving Father—promised to us by His Son. God is giving you wisdom today that will surmount any problem.

Isaiah 11:2 - The Spirit of the Lord will rest on him - the Spirit of wisdom and of understanding, the Spirit of counsel and of might, the Spirit of the knowledge and fear of the Lord. (NIV)

~

June 17 - It's Time

God knows your hidden weakness. He's not mad at you. He loves you no matter what. He does not bring up your past. He only wants to encourage all that He put into you for a divine purpose on Earth that is such a gift to you and others. Stop running. Just give Him that hidden weakness. Just let Him love you through it. No big deal to Him. Big deal to you.

Psalm 139:7-10 - Where can I go from your Spirit? Where can I flee from your presence? If I go up to the heavens, you are there; if I make my bed in the depths, you are there. If I rise on the wings of the dawn, if I settle on the far side of the sea, even there your hand will guide me, your right hand will hold me fast. (NIV)

Psalm 139:23-24 - God, I invite Your searching gaze into my heart. Examine me, find out everything that may be hidden within me. Put me to the test, and sift through all my anxious cares. See if there is any path of pain I'm walking on, and lead me back to Your glorious, everlasting ways—The path that brings me back to You. (TPT)

~

June 18 - An Excited God

If you haven't given your life to God yet, it's okay. He loves you still. He knows you will someday. So, this is for the eternal part of you that is with you now and forever. You will come to Him, and your spirit will find the Papa it has longed for—and you will be home—just as if your own family is welcoming you for Thanksgiving after a long time away. There is nothing like it. I am excited for you to experience that! And so is He.

John 3:16 - For God so loved the world that He gave His one and only Son, that whoever believes in Him should not perish but have eternal life.

~

June 19 - Just Like a Dad

What makes God sad? Well, I think He gets sad like any loving parent when their child goes wandering into trouble. We as parents know there is a better way, but our kids have to discover that way on their own sometimes. There is great joy and celebration on the day when our children turn toward all that makes them safe and happy. That makes Papa God happy, too.

Luke 15:22-24 – "But the father wasn't listening. He was calling to the servants, 'Quick. Bring a clean set of clothes and dress him. Put the family ring on his finger and sandals on his feet. Then get a prize-winning heifer and roast it. We're going to feast! We're going to have a wonderful time! My son is here —given up for dead and now alive! Given up for lost and now found!' And they began to have a wonderful time." (From the story about the prodigal son and the extravagant father. MSG)

~

June 20 - Choose Joy

God is a happy guy. We know that because we're made in His image and *we* are happy. We enjoy what He created for us. Flowers, children, music, art, dancing, puppies, kittens, wine, football, mountains, brooks, and celebrations make us happy. We're created to be joy-filled. It's in our genes.

Nehemiah 8:10 - "...the joy of the Lord is your strength." (NIV)

~

June 21 - So Dream Big!

Your dreams are coming true—the good ones— the ones full of love and life; excitement and adventure. God has heard the desires of your heart. He wants to give them to you because He put them there.

Psalm 37:4 - Delight yourself also in the Lord, and He shall give you the desires of your heart. (NKJV)

~

June 22 – Wisdom for Your Friend

There is wisdom in the words you are giving a friend today. God is preparing them to hear you and to receive your words. You are such a gift to them.

James 1:5 - If any of you lacks wisdom, you should ask God, who gives generously to all without finding fault, and it will be given you. (NIV)

~

June 23 - Make Way for the New

When I was a child, I couldn't stand the bitterness of coffee. As an adult, a grandma, I pretty much thrive on the hot flavor and need it in my morning. Something I once detested is now beautiful to me. Life is like that. We change. There are new seasons throughout our lives. It's okay to leave the old and embrace the new. As we usher in summer, let's also welcome more new beginnings on the horizon.

Ecclesiastes 3:11 - He has made everything beautiful in its time.

~

June 24 - Love Is a Wise Teacher

There are mentors, teachers, authors, and others in your life who have influenced you in a good way. Be sure to appreciate them. But know that you, too, are wise to someone else. You mentor others through just being who you are. Your love is a wise teacher.

Proverbs 3:13 – Blessed is the one who finds wisdom, and the one who gets understanding. (ESV)

~

June 25 - Forward Momentum

Days pass, and with them, time marches on in our lives toward purpose, life changes, education, and new relationships. You are sensing that now. Instead of resisting it, accept it with grace and assurance that your Papa in Heaven is with you at every moment, every step of the way. Like your best fan, He is cheering you on to greatness—and picking you up and dusting you off when you stumble. It's all part of His divine plan for you. He's so excited!

Matthew 1:23 - ...they will call him Immanuel" (which means "God with us"). (NIV)

Psalm 46:5 - God is within her, she will not fall; God will help her at break of day. (NIV)

Psalm 37:24 - Though he may stumble, he will not fall, for the Lord upholds him with his hand, (NIV)

~

June 26 - No Greater

"Shower the people you love with love, show them the way that you feel..."—the music and beautiful voice of James Taylor echoed from the towering rocks at Red Rocks Amphitheater and made me feel one with humanity. God is singing something like that over us right now. You read it in the Psalms, hear it in music; feel it in family; and exhilarate in its joy that you witness in nature. It is a bigger reality than the negative thing coming at you. Give the good things your total attention.

John 15:13 - Greater love has no one than this: to lay down one's life for one's friends. (NIV)

~

June 27 - His Sun Shines Upon Us All

As a mountain girl now living in a big city, I have been encountered twice by people I'm not used to. It is drawing out a side of me I thought I had dealt with. How do I respond to their needy requests? Well, I didn't do so well. I responded from fear I think, when I really needed wisdom for discernment. Who do I help? When should I be kind? When do I deny them to protect myself? I know I am to always love and be compassionate. I'm still working on this. Today, God is giving us all wisdom on how to love better and also wisdom on how to discern His heart in a situation.

Matthew 5:44-46 - But I tell you, love your enemies and pray for those who persecute you, that you may be children of your Father in heaven. He causes his sun to rise on the evil and the good, and sends rain on the righteous and the unrighteous. If you love those who love you, what reward will you get? Are not even the tax collectors doing that? (NIV)

Matthew 5:45 - This is what God does. He gives his best—the sun to warm and the rain to nourish—to everyone, regardless... (MSG).

James 1:5 - And if anyone longs to be wise, ask God for wisdom and he will give it! He won't see your lack of wisdom as an opportunity to scold you over your failures but he will overwhelm your failures with his generous grace. (TPT)

~

June 28 - Visit Your Power Place

There are physical places on Earth that have power for us. As a writer, I feel more creative in certain coffee shops, book shops, and parks. As a photographer, my soul is filled on a mountain trail with distant views and the scent of pine. It's as if the earth and all of Creation are demonstrating their love for you in that place! Where is your power place? Be sure to spend time there and renew your spirit and your sense of purpose.

Romans 8:19 - The entire universe waits with excitement, yearning to see the unveiling of God's glorious sons and daughters! (TPT)

Jeremiah 10:12 – But it is God whose power made the earth, whose wisdom gave shape to the world, who crafted the cosmos. (MSG)

~

June 29 – Work on Your Dream

What is it you have always wanted to do? To learn? To explore? This is the day to work on that. Take a step. Check out a book. Plan an itinerary. Sign up for a class. Research a possibility. Declare yourself that person that does that thing. I am a writer. I am a photographer. I am brilliant. I travel the world. I have climbed that mountain. I am a realtor. I am a nurse. I am a teacher. I am a brilliant businessperson. I can build a house. I'm fast. I'm strong. I am going to win that contest. Your buried dreams are ready for new life. It's time.

Psalm 90:17 - May the favor of the Lord our God rest on us; establish the work of our hands for us—yes, establish the work of our hands. (NIV)

Job 22:28 – You will also declare a thing and it will be established for you; so light will shine on your ways. (NKJV)

June 30 - Your Tapestry Will Help Someone

Just as a tapestry is made more beautiful because of its contrasting colors and textures, so our life is more beautiful as we age because of our experiences—both good and bad; easy and difficult. Look at your life so far. Do you see how your faith has grown? Do you see how you have been loved and protected? Nothing can give you that like experience can. Today you will encourage someone else, and they will trust what you say because they see in you the beauty and truth that experience has given you.

Romans 8:28 - And we know that all things work together for good to those who love God, to those who are the called according to His purpose. (NKJV)

Psalm 92:12-15 - The righteous will flourish like a palm tree, they will grow like a cedar of Lebanon; planted in the house of the Lord, they will flourish in the courts of our God. They will still bear fruit in old age, they will stay fresh and green, proclaiming, "The Lord is upright; he is my Rock, and there is no wickedness in him." (NIV)

July

July

July 1 - What's the Story?

There are so many different kinds of writers. There are teachers, dreamers, philosophers, songwriters, poets, musicians, screenwriters, and journalists, all with creative gifts stemming from their own experiences. We as readers critique from our own life experiences that have shaped our thoughts, morals, and values. I'm an editor. How in the world do I edit that? My highest core values for coaching writers are—stay on point, use the best words, and simply tell the story. Take out all else that distracts from the story. Period.

Our life is rather like this. What is our point? Our story? Our goal? Take out all else that distracts from that. Period.

Psalm 20:4 - May he give you the desire of your heart and make all your plans succeed. (NIV)

~

July 2 - See Heaven on Earth

I love to hike with my camera. It's a pal, really. It helps me be more aware of my surroundings. It serves as a brain to my eyes. Without the camera, I see at 60 percent. With it, I see more than 100 percent. There are such surprises around every turn. What is your lens? What helps you "see"? It can be physical like a camera or journal ... or it can be abstract like simple joy. There is more meaning to our life that lies beyond or just underneath what we perceive with our five senses. Expect to experience that today.

Romans 1:20 - But the basic reality of God is plain enough. Open your eyes and there it is! By taking a long and thoughtful look at what God has created, people have always been able to see what their eyes as such can't see: eternal power, for instance, and the mystery of his divine being. (MSG)

July 3 - Father Knows What's Going On

From God's perspective, our world is doing pretty much what He always knew it would. That's why He sent Jesus. He knew we would need a savior from ourselves. We are not in a hopeless situation—ever. He is a kind, loving, generous, giving, good Father. He wants you to know that.

You're a good, good Father.

It's who you are, it's who you are, it's who you are,

And I am loved by you.

It's who I am, it's who I am, it's who I am."

(From a song called "Good, Good Father" by Housefires.)

~

July 4 - Step into Victory

Today—step into victory. What is holding you back? Laugh at that. And let go of it. Step forward. Take a chance. Enter your dreams, your destiny, and your purpose. You are not alone if your Friend is the Creator of the Universe. He IS your success! Go for it.

Ephesians 6:10 – Now my beloved ones, I have saved these most important truths for last: Be supernaturally infused with strength through your life-union with the Lord Jesus. Stand victorious with the force of his explosive power flowing in and through you. (TPT)

~

July 5 - What Is Your Oasis?

Find your oasis. Is it a coffee shop? A backyard? By a stream? In a book? Atop a horse? Enter solace and peace. Rest today.

Oasis - 1. A small fertile or green area in a desert region, usually having a spring or well. 2. Something serving as a refuge, relief, or pleasant change from what is usual, annoying, difficult, etc. (Dictionary.com)

Isaiah 26:3 – You will keep him in perfect peace, whose mind is stayed on You, because he trusts in You. (NKJV)

~

July 6 - The Lord's Face

I look at my pansies, and their cute "faces" always cheer my spirit. There are "faces" in a lot of natural things, like clouds, rocks, and other flowers. Let it be a reminder of God's care for you. His face shines on you. He is so proud of you, His child.

Numbers 6:24-26 - "The Lord bless you and keep you; the Lord make his face shine on you and be gracious to you; the Lord turn his face toward you and give you peace." (NIV)

~

July 7 - Go

Butterflies are a prophetic sign of freedom. This is your day to be like a butterfly—to fly above; to change your life; to begin anew; and to be free. Prepare for take-off.

2 Corinthians 5:17 – Therefore, if anyone is in Christ, he is a new creation, the old has gone, the new has come! (NIV)

~

July 8 - Hooray

You celebrate anniversaries with joy and good memories. Do you know there are new anniversaries coming? Yes! You will celebrate the anniversaries of new jobs, the day you were healed, the day you had the financial breakthrough, and the day your grandchild was born. So much more is ahead.

Psalm 128:1-2 - All you who fear God, how blessed you are! How happily you walk on his smooth straight road! You worked hard and deserve all you've got coming. Enjoy the blessing! Revel in the goodness! (MSG)

~

July 9 - A Gift of Knowing

Today you are being given a gift of discernment. You will see and know the truth about a situation so you can make a wise decision.

Jeremiah 33:3 - Call to me and I will answer you, and will tell you great and hidden things that you have not known. (ESV)

~

July 10 - Exciting Times Coming

New friends and relationships are on the horizon. Oh, what an exciting time is coming soon. It reminds me of a song I sang in Girl Scouts. “Make new friends but keep the old. One is silver and the other gold.” Embrace this time of connection.

1 Corinthians 2:9 - "Eye has not seen, nor ear heard, nor have entered into the heart of man the things which God has prepared for those who love Him." (NKJV)

~

July 11 - What Is Beautiful to You?

Take the watercolor class, buy the piece of art, wear the new, colorful, shirt. Today is a day to celebrate your love for beauty and creativity.

Exodus 31:2-4 -Then the Lord said to Moses, "See, I have chosen Bezalel son of Uri, the son of Hur, of the tribe of Judah, and I have filled him with the Spirit of God, with wisdom, with understanding, with knowledge and with all kinds of skills - to make artistic designs for work in gold, silver and bronze, to cut and set stones, to work in wood, and to engage in all kinds of crafts.

~

July 12 - A Child Will Bless You

A child will bless your heart today in ways you cannot conceive or imagine. Watch for the deeper meaning in what she or he is doing and saying. Let them know how special they are.

Isaiah 11:6 - And a little child will lead them. (NIV)

Psalm 127:3 - Don't you see that children are God's best gift? (MSG)

Matthew 18:10 - "For I tell you that their angels in heaven always see the face of my Father in heaven." (NIV)

~

July 13 - Intentional Health

Your health is a gift to you. Be sure to take care of you today. Make the appointment, take a walk, gaze at something beautiful, breathe, laugh, call someone you love. Accept God's invitation to sit on a rock with Him.

3 John 1:2 - Dear friend, I pray that you may enjoy good health and that all may go well with you, even as your soul is getting along well. (NIV)

Proverbs 17:22 - A joyful heart is good medicine. (ESV)

~

July 14 - Sing

Sing that song on your heart. Sing with abandon. Sing loud with joy ... in the shower, in the car, with your kids, or from the mountaintop. It's a day to lift your voice in joy for all the blessings you have.

Isaiah 51:11 - Those the Lord has rescued will return. They will enter Zion with singing; everlasting joy will crown their heads. Gladness and joy will overtake them, and sorrow and sighing will flee away. (NIV)

Psalm 63:5 - I will be fully satisfied as with the richest of foods; with singing lips my mouth will praise you.

~

July 15 - Extreme Strength

Some people are strong physically. For others, their strength is in their quiet nature. Still others think they are weak when they are vulnerable, but God wants you to know extreme strength develops from that vulnerability. Do not be afraid to be yourself.

2 Corinthians 12:9 - But he said to me, "My grace is sufficient for you, for my power is made perfect in weakness." (NIV)

~

July 16 - Enlarge the Important

Cropping is taking out of a photo the things that don't add to the photo—bringing into view the part that will tell the story the best. Are there some things that need to be cropped out of your life to bring it into better focus?

Philippians 3:13-14 - Brethren, I do not count myself to have apprehended; but one thing I do, forgetting those things which are behind and reaching forward to those things which are ahead, I press toward the goal for the prize of the upward call of God in Christ Jesus. (NKJV)

~

July 17 - God Loves the Internet

Technology is a gift to the world. Don't let fear let you think it is bad. Also, know that you have authority over how you will use it and how you will be blessed by it. God loves technology. It's all about spreading His love as far as it can go and reaching people where they are. The internet is a good tool. Use it today to bless another.

Acts 1:8 - "But you will receive power when the Holy Spirit comes on you; and you will be my witnesses in Jerusalem, and in all Judea and Samaria, and to the ends of the earth." (NIV)

Romans 1:11 - I long to see you so that I may impart to you some spiritual gift to make you strong. (NIV)

~

July 18 - Limitless Love

Do you know just how much God loves you? If you were the only person in the world, He couldn't love you more. That love is in you for others, too. Let it go forth.

1 John 4:19 – We love because He first loved us. (ESV)

~

July 19 - Family

Families can look different to each of us. Big, small, funny, serious, a bit nutty, sometimes troubling. God is asking you to love bigger today. How will that look for you?

"Family and friendships are two of the greatest facilitators of happiness." — John C. Maxwell

Psalm 68:6 – God sets the lonely in families. (NIV)

~

July 20 - Can You Hear?

The daily words in this book are Father God's heart for your day—written after prayer for each day. God loves you so and wants you to know these things. He will speak to you, too. Just pray. Ask Him what you want to know. Then listen to the first thoughts. Be aware of your surroundings. He speaks to us through lots of things—like nature, friends, books, the Bible, thoughts, dreams, and coincidences.

Psalm 119:105 - Your word is a lamp for my feet, and a light on my path. (NKJV)

James 4:8 - Come near to God and he will come near to you. (NIV)

~

July 21 - Stir Your Spirit

What is your favorite color, shape, sound, or song? Today, mine are yellow, heart, birds, and a song called "No Longer Slaves" by Bethel Music. God created sights and sounds, colors and music to stir our souls and spirits. Embrace your favorites today.

Proverbs 15:13 - A happy heart makes the face cheerful ... (NIV)

~

July 22 - All Hope

If something is trying to bring you down—don't let it. Say no. Faith is hope in what isn't seen— trust in the One who is able. There is all hope.

Psalm 25:5 – Guide me in your truth and teach me, for you are God my Savior, and my hope is in you all day long. (NIV)

Hebrews 11:1 - The fundamental fact of existence is that this trust in God, this faith, is the firm foundation under everything that makes life worth living. It's our handle on what we can't see. The act of faith is what distinguished our ancestors, set them above the crowd. (MSG)

~

July 23 - It's Personal

We look up at the sky and see and hear high-flying jets. Those pilots look down, and they don't see us. They have a greater perspective. But God isn't like that. We can look up with our spirit and sense His Presence. We can perceive Him in nature through the things He created. And He promises that He sees us, too. He's a big, big God —able to relate to each of His kids as if we are unique and special—because He says we are.

Psalm 139:16-17 - All the days ordained for me were written in your book before one of them came to be. How precious to me are your thoughts, God! How vast is the sum of them! (NIV)

~

July 24 - Watch for Good to Come

Did you know that God doesn't waste anything? Our experiences, big and small, good and bad—He will use to bless us and bless others. Look back on your life. Can you see the good that came from a hard experience? If not, ask God to help you see. He is bringing good out of the difficulty you are having today. Broken relationships yield to better ones. Lost jobs make room for better ones. Even the loss of a loved one will help you recognize how much you were able to love. And financial ruin can turn around and set you in a new direction that is more fun and more profitable in many ways. Trust the process. Even if you can't trust yet, God will still bring out the good.

Romans 8:28 - So we are convinced that every detail of our lives is continually woven together to fit into God's perfect plan of bringing good into our lives, for we are his lovers who have been called to fulfill his designed purpose. (TPT)

Romans 8:31 - If God has determined to stand with us, tell me, who then could ever stand against us? (TPT)

~

July 25 - Set New Blessings in Motion

Being thankful today for what you have is far greater than worrying about what you don't have yet. Your thankfulness will set new blessings into motion.

Philippians 4:6-7 - Don't be pulled in different directions or worried about a thing. Be saturated in prayer throughout each day, offering your faith-filled requests before God with overflowing gratitude. Tell Him every detail of your life, then God's wonderful peace that transcends human understanding, will guard your heart and mind through Jesus Christ. (TPT)

July 26 - Fear Not

When it hails, just think, "All Hail the Power."

When it rains, just think, "Rain down your blessings."

When it thunders, just think, "Thank you that the rain is coming."

When the lightning comes, just think, "God you are so amazing!"

We need not fear the storms in our life. Fear isn't from God. Rejoice in everything.

Psalm 91: 4, 6, 9 - His arms of faithfulness are a shield keeping you from harm. Don't fear a thing! When we live our lives within the shadow of God Most High, our secret hiding place, we will always be shielded from harm! (TPT)

July 27 - Signs in the Sky

When you see a rainbow, remember God promises to keep all of His promises. His answers to us are "Yes!" He is for us, not against us. He is our greatest cheerleader.

Psalm 89:34 - My covenant I will not break; nor alter the word that has gone out of my lips. (NKJV)

July 28 On Target for Greatness

Sometimes I like to wear a hat when I write. It helps me to be more creative. Whatever works! What props help you get into who you were created to be? A latté? A purple-colored wall? Your desk organized just so? A little mascara? Those favorite boots? Ripped jeans? It's okay. We are human. Get your prop and get going into whatever today is bringing. You are on target.

Genesis 1:31 - God saw all that he had made, and it was very good. (NIV)

~

July 29 Alter Your Creativity Today

When we bought our Denver home, my favorite part of it was the scraggly confusion of bushes crossing the back of the property. In my imagination, I could see a great series of rooms and tunnels and paths in those bushes—perfect for a fort. Well, grandson Trey saw that, too, and we now have a very refined "Kid Cave" that I imagine all the grands will enjoy. Look at your place and life. What new thing is your imagination telling you about a corner of it? Creativity in a different form will stimulate your creativity in your work and gifts. Have fun.

"Every child is an artist. The problem is staying an artist when you grow up." Pablo Picasso

~

July 30 – Step into More

There is such freedom in knowing who you are and knowing you were created for a reason. Today you will experience more joy than you have ever experienced before, because you will be closer to knowing who you really are.

Psalm 44:3 – You loved to give them victory, for you took great delight in them. (TPT)

~

July 31 - Your Heart's Desire

In their imaginations, my little grandchildren really are mommies, champion barrel racers, professional baseball players, and wonderful artists. As adults, we need to be like them. What is your imagination telling you about who you are? There is still all hope and promise to become your heart's desire for yourself.

Psalm 49:3 - 4 – For wisdom will come from my mouth; words of insight and understanding will be heard from the musings of my heart. I will break open mysteries with my music, and my song will release riddles solved.

August

August

August 1 - Can You Hear?

Have you heard God talk? One time I heard Him when I had to make a big decision whether to attend ministry school for a second year. I had asked God what I should do and wouldn't budge on my decision until I was sure I heard from Him. One day, sitting outside of my apartment, I heard a voice in my imagination say, "You're only half-baked and I need you well done." Whoa! I don't say things like that or even think things like that. I knew right away it was God's answer. And He was funny! Today He is speaking to you, too. Can you hear Him? He will help you with your decision if you ask Him.

Psalm 50:1 - The mighty One, God, the Lord Himself has spoken! He shouts out over all the people of the earth, in every brilliant sunrise and every beautiful sunset, saying "Listen to Me!" (TPT)

~

August 2 - Kick Back

Some days our bodies are telling us to be still. Today is a day like that. Kick back. Read a book. Pray. Listen. That is all.

Psalm 23:2-3 – He offers a resting place for me in his luxurious love. His tracks take me to an oasis of peace, the quiet brook of bliss. That's where he restores and revives my life. (TPT)

~

August 3 - Supercharged Life

Our bodies are such a miracle. No matter our age, we are designed to heal. A doctor can set a bone or prescribe medicine, but our bodies do what they were created to do. They mend, rebuild, and support our life. There is no illness in Heaven. We are perfectly created, and that should be our experience on Earth as it is in Heaven. So, declare that today. Declare health over your body, mind, and spirit. Thank you, God!

Psalm 103:1-6 - With my whole heart, with my whole life, and with my innermost being, I bow in wonder and love before You, the Holy God! Yahweh, You are my soul's celebration, how could I ever forget the miracles of kindness You've done for me? You've kissed my heart with Your forgiveness, in spite of all I've done! You've healed me inside and out from every disease! You've rescued me from hell and saved my life! You've crowned me with love and mercy and made me a king! You satisfy my every desire with good things! You've supercharged my life so that I soar again like a flying eagle in the sky! (TPT)

~

August 4 - People Need Your Fruit

The fruits of the Spirit are what communicate God's love through us to others. You are a conveyor of those fruits—demonstrating them, encouraging with them, teaching them. You are so good at this! The fruits are love, joy, peace, forbearance, kindness, goodness, faithfulness, gentleness, and self-control.

Galatians 5:22-23 - But what happens when we live God's way? He brings gifts into our lives, much the same way that fruit appears in an orchard - things like affection for others, exuberance about life, serenity. We develop a willingness to stick with things, a sense of compassion in the heart, and a conviction that a basic holiness permeates things and people. We find ourselves involved in loyal commitments, not needing to force our way in life, able to marshal and direct our energies wisely. (MSG)

~

August 5 - Songs of Joy

Step outside and listen. What do you hear? In the midst of the hustle and bustle of life, can you gear down and hear nature? A trickling stream or the rustle of leaves in the breeze? The chatter of a squirrel or the happy squeal of a toddler? Today, be so thankful for a beautiful creation that not only excites your sense of vision, taste, and smell—but also has sounds that fill you with wonder. It will keep you open to the new blessing God is about to give you.

Psalm 65:8 - The whole earth is filled with awe at your wonders; where morning dawns, where evening fades, you call forth songs of joy. (NIV)

~

August 6 - Coffee and Wisdom

Today, make a perfect cup of coffee or your favorite drink, and take a few minutes alone to sit outside and have a chat with your Creator. Ask Him what He thinks of you. Ask Him the question that has been on your heart. Ask Him what He plans to do about it. He is relational. Don't be afraid. He's ready to help you.

Psalm 109:4 – I will pray until I become prayer itself. (TPT)

Psalm 138:3 – At the very moment I called out to you, you answered me! You strengthened me deep within my soul. (TPT)

~

August 7 - Job Well Done

An award or diploma is headed your way for something you have worked hard for. You will be recognized.

Colossians 3:23 - Whatever you do, work at it with all your heart, as working for the Lord, not for human masters. (NIV)

Ephesians 6:7-8 - Serve wholeheartedly, as if you were serving the Lord, not people, because you know that the Lord will reward each one for whatever good they do, whether they are slave or free. (NIV)

August 8 - Your Reward

Be diligent in doing good, even if no one seems to notice. Your Father in Heaven is noticing. Your reward will be greater than you can imagine.

Galatians 6:9 - And don't allow yourselves to be weary or disheartened in planting good seeds, for the season of reaping the wonderful harvest you've planted is coming! (TPT)

~

August 9 - It's a Birth-Day

Give birth today to the new thing that is on your heart and mind to do. God is blessing it. Not only will it bless you, but others will be blessed by what you do, too.

2 Corinthians 9:8 - And God is able to make all grace abound toward you, that you, always having all sufficiency in all things, may have an abundance for every good work. (NKJV)

~

August 10 - Breakthrough

There is breakthrough today in something you have been waiting for. Just as a carrot is one of the last things to germinate in your salad garden, so is the seed you have been carrying and nurturing for a long time. You will celebrate very soon.

Psalm 139:3-4 – You are so intimately aware of me, Lord. You read my heart like an open book...you've gone into my future to prepare the way and in kindness you follow behind me to spare me from the harm of my past. With your hand of love upon my life, you impart a blessing to me. (TPT)

~

August 11 - Dream Life

Your night dreams are more vivid lately. God is speaking to you during these times and downloading what you need: wisdom, answers, and ideas. Pay attention and write them down when you think of them.

Daniel 1:17 - To these four young men God gave knowledge and understanding of all kinds of literature and learning. And Daniel could understand visions and dreams of all kinds.

~

August 12 - Good Remedies

Do you ever feel a little off kilter? A bit out of tune? You need a day to refresh. Only a bit of creativity, quiet, and joy can remedy you. Have fun.

"Art washes away from the soul the dust of everyday life." Pablo Picasso

Ecclesiastes 3:1 - To everything there is a season, a time for every purpose under heaven. (NKJV)

~

August 13 - Never Alone

New to Denver after almost a lifetime in the quieter mountains, I am beginning to get accustomed to loud night noises. Sirens, distant trains, and unmuffled cars and motorcycles have been alarming me in the middle of the night. But I must dial down, mentally calm my nerves, and intentionally quiet myself. God wants us to remember to be still and know He is there.

Psalm 46:7, 10 - The Mighty Lord of Angel-Armies is on our side! The God of Jacob fights for us! Surrender your anxiety! (Excerpts from TPT)

August 14 - A Tiny Adjustment!

My piano had a huge problem of a key that would not work. The piano tuner discovered it had been weighted with a piece of lead by another technician who had attempted to fix it. Upon very close examination, he discovered a tiny bolt that had been twisted ever so slightly. With a simple adjustment and removal of the lead weight, the problem was solved. Chances are you have a problem like that. It looks big, but upon close examination, you will discover the tiny adjustment that will make everything right.

Psalm 119:130 – Break open your word within me until revelation-light shines out! (TPT)

Psalm 70:5 – Lord, in my place of weakness and need, won't you turn your heart toward me and hurry to help me? For you are my Savior and I'm always in your thoughts. (TPT)

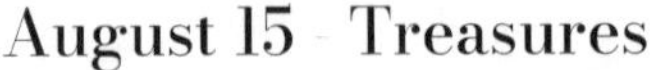

August 15 - Treasures

God is releasing new and old treasures into your life. What fun it will be to journal what you think these might be.

Psalm 67:7 – And the blessings keep coming! (TPT)

~

August 16 - The Great Price

God wants you to remember the price He paid for your freedom. It keeps you humble, and in that humility is great strength to survive this amazing life and destiny He has given you.

John 3:16 - For God so loved the world that he gave his one and only Son, that whoever believes in him shall not perish but have eternal life.

Ephesians 2:10 - We become His poetry, a recreated people that will fulfill the destiny He has given each of us, (TPT)

2 Corinthians 3:17 - Now the Lord is the Spirit, and where the Spirit of the Lord is, there is freedom. (NIV)

~

August 17 - Surround Your Life with Goodness

My house is a mix of very old and somewhat new construction and décor. I like that. There is something that speaks to my every mood and memory. What speaks to you? Surround yourself with things that speak goodness, hope, beauty, joy, and love.

Psalm 23:6 - Surely your goodness and love will follow me all the days of my life, and I will dwell in the house of the Lord forever. (TPT)

Lamentations 3:22-23 - Because of the Lord's great love we are not consumed, for his compassions never fail. They are new every morning; great is your faithfulness. (NIV)

~

August 18 - Change an Atmosphere

Do you know you can change an atmosphere? Try it. Change a negative conversation to something positive. Bring laughter to a lonely group of people. Your beautiful self is designed to bring hope to others. Today, you will be an atmosphere changer.

1 Thessalonians 5:11 - Therefore encourage one another and build each other up, just as in fact you are doing. (NIV)

Proverbs 16:24 - Gracious words are a honeycomb, sweet to the soul and healing to the bones. (NIV)

~

August 19 - Happy Filters

I love Monet paintings and have a few framed prints in my home. I love the artist's soft, dreamy, colors and landscapes, the rich brush strokes, and the light that shines from his images. The scenes make me feel peaceful, as if I'm in the painting itself. I have a Monet type of filter for many of my life memories. It's a happy thing. What is your happy filter? You will use it today to help you deal with something, to help you see the beauty and goodness in it.

Philippians 1:9 - I continue to pray for your love to grow and increase beyond measure, bringing you into the rich revelation of spiritual insight in all things. (TPT)

~

August 20 The Language of Life

I've been watching the squirrels in my yard, and I think that, in addition to their chatter, they have a tail language. Like squirrels, we say things with our voice, but we also communicate with the language of our life. Today, you will see how you can encourage others when they watch how you model life.

Psalm 97:11 - Light shines on the righteous and joy on the upright in heart.

~

August 21 Intentionally Happy

My little granddaughter was born yesterday, wasn't she? And now she just started Middle School. Time moves on so quickly. Make it happy for yourself and for those around you. Happiness can be an intentional thing. You are blessed to be a blessing.

Psalm 42:6-8 - Then God promises to love me all day, sing songs all through the night! My life is God's prayer. (Excerpt from MSG)

Psalm 5:3 – Every morning I lay out the pieces of my life on the altar and wait for your fire to fall upon my heart. (TPT)

August 22 – Older and Wiser

When I was given a beautiful 1948 Baldwin piano, I was amazed at how pretty it sounded even though it had not been tuned for many years. The original craftsmanship and quality of materials helped it last over all this time. The Creator made humans that way, too, with quality craftsmanship. We are meant to get even better with age because of the gifts of wisdom, grace, patience, and love. (Fine tuning helps, too.)

Psalm 92:14-15 – Even in their old age they will stay fresh, bearing luscious fruit and abiding faithfully. Listen to them! With pleasure they still proclaim: "You're so good! You're my beautiful strength! You've never made a mistake with me." (TPT)

Wrinkles should merely indicate where smiles have been. - Mark Twain

August 23 - Walking with Sparkle

People will be drawn to you today. It is because you are shiny!

John 8:12 - When Jesus spoke again to the people, he said, "I am the light of the world. Whoever follows me will never walk in darkness, but will have the light of life." (NIV)

Psalm 34:5 – Gaze upon him, join your life with his, and joy will come. Your faces will glisten with glory... (TPT)

~

August 24 - Our Hiding Place

Do you know you are hidden, safe, protected, and loved? God promises to shelter us. Remember you are never alone!

Psalm 91:4 - His massive arms are wrapped around you, protecting you. You can run under His covering of majesty and hide. His arms of faithfulness are a shield keeping you from harm. (TPT)

Psalm 32:7 - You are my hiding place; you will protect me from trouble and surround me with songs of deliverance. (NIV)

Hebrews 13:6 - So we can confidently say, "The Lord is my helper; I will not fear; what can man do to me?" (ESV)

~

August 25 - Surprise!

Something surprising is about to happen, and it will be surprisingly good!

Psalm 23:6 – So why would I fear the future? Only goodness and tender love pursue me all the days of my life. Then afterward—when my life is through—I'll return to Your glorious presence to be forever with You! (TPT)

James 1:17 - Every good and perfect gift is from above, coming down from the Father of the heavenly lights, who does not change like shifting shadows. (NIV)

~

August 26 – A Reward is Coming

It's a day of recompense. You will be compensated in some way for a task or act you did in the past that you thought had been forgotten.

Proverbs 12:14 – "For there is great satisfaction in speaking the truth, and hard work brings blessings back to you. (TPT)

~

August 27 - Fresh Focus

Some idea or new adventure is taking flight today and coming into focus.

Matthew 19:26 – Jesus looked at them and said, "With man this is impossible, but with God, all things are possible."

~

August 28 - Clarity

The pressure you feel from life right now is lifting, and soon you will see more of what you are meant to do.

Proverbs 16:9 – Within your heart you can make plans for your future, but the Lord chooses the steps you take to get there. (TPT)

August 29 - Quiet in Spirit

Even on a busy workday, you are learning to be quiet in your spirit and mind, and are beginning to hear more from your Father in Heaven.

Psalm 119:114 – You're my place of quiet retreat, and your wrap-around presence becomes my shield as I wrap myself in your word. (TPT)

August 30 - Patience Rewarded

Something that aggravates you is being dealt with right now. Your patience with it will be rewarded.

Hebrews 6:12 - ...Be like those who stay the course with committed faith and then get everything promised to them. (MSG)

August 31 - First Things First

In a world that is chaotic, there is an order. When you seek God first, all other things will line up and you will have peace, understanding, and favor.

Matthew 6:33 - But seek first his kingdom and his righteousness, and all these things will be given to you as well. (NIV)

September

September

September 1 - Changing Seasons

Cloud formations, rain, and sunlight angles are announcing a change of seasons in the natural. They are also signaling a change of seasons in the spirit realm. Watch, wait, and be aware. Expect and anticipate good things ahead.

Ezekiel 34:26 - I will make them and the places surrounding my hill a blessing. I will send down showers in season; there will be showers of blessing. (NIV)

~

September 2 - Listen for God's Voice

God is asking you to slow down. To just breathe. To stop talking so much and start listening. Prayer is good. Listening for His voice is even better. You will hear Him.

Proverbs 3 - Trust God from the bottom of your heart; don't try to figure out everything on your own. Listen for God's voice in everything you do, everywhere you go; he's the one who will keep you on track. (MSG)

~

September 3 - We Are Not Alone

Things are lining up for you. Numbers seem to have some significance. On the clock. On license plates. 3:33; 5:55, 11:11. Know that they mean something for you—if for no other reason than to let you know you are not alone. God is with you and knows what you're going through.

Joshua 1:9 - Have I not commanded you? Be strong and courageous. Do not be frightened, and do not be dismayed, for the Lord your God is with you wherever you go. (ESV)

~

September 4 - Sure Victory

When you are stuck, walk forward with your Father God and break down the walls confining you. God is for you. He has a plan for you, and you have already entered it.

Psalm 107:28 – Then we cried out, "Lord, help us! Rescue us!" And He did! (TPT)

Romans 8:31 - If God is for us, who can be against us? (ESV)

~

September 5 - Unique You

Just as each bird has its own special song, each human has a special imprint they make. Your voice, your appearance, and your thumbprint are uniquely yours. Your destiny and purpose are unique to you, too. Today you will have a greater awareness of your giftedness.

Ephesians 2:10 - For we are God's handiwork, created in Christ Jesus to do good works, which God prepared in advance for us to do.

~

September 6 - So Good

Can you see that everything you have experienced in life—the good, the bad, the dreams achieved, the skills learned, relationships, people connections, and adventures— have culminated in the person you are and the life you have today? Stay the course and watch His good continue to unfold for you in areas of your dreams, business, and relationships.

Proverbs 8:35 - For those who find me find life and receive favor from the Lord. (NIV)

~

September 7 - It'll Be Wild!

Your adventurous spirit is about to get a big present. It's going to be fun. It's going to be wild. There's nothing more you can do to be ready for it. Just watch. Wait for it, then enter in.

"Twenty years from now you will be more disappointed by the things that you didn't do than by the ones you did do. So throw off the bowlines. Sail away from the safe harbor. Catch the trade winds in your sails. Explore. Dream. Discover." ~ Mark Twain

"Only those who will risk going too far can possibly find out how far one can go." ~ T. S. Eliot

~

September 8 - Spiritual Bug Repellent

Crickets chirping on summer nights are rather pleasant, like a lullaby. But a cricket in the kitchen is another creepy, loud, sleepless story. Be sure to surround your life with prayer and declare the promises of God's protection, knowing angels have your back. That ought to keep the "bugs" outside.

Psalm 91:1 – When you abide under the shadow of Shaddai, you are hidden in the strength of God Most High. (TPT)

Psalm 91:9-10 – For everyone who knows your wonderful name keeps putting their trust in you. They can count on you for help no matter what. O Lord, you will never, no never, neglect those who come to you. (TPT)

Psalm 91:11 - God will send His messenger angels with special orders to protect you wherever you go, defending you from all harm. (TPT)

~

September 9 - Ready? Leap!

A life of risk is not reckless. It is a life fully trusting in a God that is able to get us where He wants to take us. Take that leap, but don't jump without Him!

"Faith does not operate in the realm of the possible. There is no glory for God in that which is humanly possible. Faith begins where man's power ends." George Mueller

~

September 10 - Make That Decision

There is an expression that haste makes waste. But stalling and riding the fence on a decision can cause anxiety, wasted time, and missed opportunity. God is calling you to make a decision on a thing that can only succeed with His help and blessing.

"The dogs of doom stand and bark at the doors of your destiny." - Kris Vallotton

Psalm 102:13 – Now is the time, Lord, for your compassion and mercy to be poured out – the appointed time has come for your prophetic promises to be fulfilled! (TPT)

~

September 11 - Fear Not

Fear is not from God. When it appears, negate it with a promise from God. Declare "no weapon formed against me shall prosper." "I am the head not the tail." "God will supply all my need." "God is my strength and my shield."

"He covers me and places me high on a rock." "He is my protector." "There is an army of angels surrounding me." Today, you are reaching new levels of boldness and strength. Go out and conquer your world.

Isaiah 41:10 - So do not fear, for I am with you; do not be dismayed, for I am your God. I will strengthen you and help you; I will uphold you with my righteous right hand. (NIV)

~

September 12 - You're Almost There

You are tempted to get off the roller coaster of life and withdraw from something that is hard for you. I just hear God saying, "Stay in the river." Flowing with His Holy Spirit is the best place to be. He is with you there. Stick with it because you have almost arrived.

Psalm 46:4 - There is a river whose streams make glad the city of God. (NIV)

~

September 13 - Ask! Ask!

In John chapter 14, Jesus repeats Himself two different times. First, he teaches us to not let our hearts be troubled and to trust in God. And then He says it again. Then He tells us He will do whatever we ask in His name. And within the same breath almost – he says it again! I think He means it. There is something you need to ask Him. Today's the day. He will do it!

Psalm 37:4 - Find your delight and true pleasure in Yahweh, and he will give you what you desire the most. (TPT)

Philippians 4:19 - I am convinced that my God will fully satisfy every need you have, for I have seen the abundant riches of glory revealed to me through Jesus Christ. (TPT)

2 Corinthians 9:8 - Yes, God is more than ready to overwhelm you with every form of grace, so that you will have more than enough of everything—every moment and in every way. He will make you overflow with abundance in every good thing you do. (TPT)

~

September 14 - Like a Wise Owl

You have asked Papa God for wisdom, and as He promised, He is giving you what you need for a situation in your life. He is also helping you see more clearly (just like an owl at night) into areas that have been hidden or in the shadows.

Proverbs 2:6 - Wisdom is a gift from a generous God, and every word he speaks is full of revelation and becomes a fountain of understanding within you. (TPT)

1 Corinthians 12:7 - Each believer is given continuous revelation by the Holy Spirit to benefit not just himself but all. (TPT)

~

September 15 - Like the First Snow

The excitement you feel at the first snow of the fall season or the first flower of spring is what you are feeling today. You know something is coming, and it's going to be fresh and beautiful.

Proverbs 23:18 - There is surely a future hope for you, and your hope will not be cut off.

~

September 16 - No Fear

Our son used to wear tee shirts and ball caps with the "No Fear" logo on them. I liked that. It was like a proclamation over his life that said, "I will fear nothing and no one!" Do you know that you have a promise over your life, too? You can walk confidently with a spiritual "No Fear" logo because you are a child of the Most High God. His power in you is your power. How cool is that?

Psalm 68:34-35 - Proclaim the power of God, whose majesty is over Israel, whose power is in the heavens. You, God, are awesome in your sanctuary; the God of Israel gives power and strength to his people. (NIV)

~

September 17 - The Father's Blessing

This is just for you today:

Numbers 6:24-26 - "The Lord bless you and keep you; the Lord make his face shine on you and be gracious to you; the Lord turn his face toward you and give you peace." (NIV)

~

September 18 - What Is Hidden for You?

We recently found a perfect zucchini hiding in our garden under its protective leaves. The funny thing is, we had no idea it was even there. God hides surprises like that for us in a spiritual way, too. He hides them for us, not from us. He delights in us going after the things He has hidden for us—things like promises, revelation, and wisdom. Today is a day of delightful discovery.

Proverbs 25:2 - God conceals the revelation of His Word in the hiding place of His glory. But the honor of kings is revealed to all by how they thoroughly mine out the deeper meaning of all that God says. (TPT)

Proverbs 25:2 - God delights in concealing things; scientists delight in discovering things. (MSG)

~

September 19 - Provision

Watch for a financial blessing.

Psalm 145:16 - You open Your hand and satisfy the desires of every living thing. (NIV)

Matthew 7:11 - If you, imperfect as you are, know how to lovingly take care of your children and give them what's best, how much more ready is your heavenly father to give wonderful gifts to those who ask him? (TPT)

~

September 20 - Hope for Relationships

In the area of matters of the heart, God wants you to know He stands with you in every relationship—to bless you and give you hope.

John 13:34 - "So I give you a new commandment: Love each other just as much as I have loved you...." (TPT)

~

September 21 - Peace He Gives to Us

Trees are turning color, and a season of peace and beauty is upon us. Today, breathe deep and enjoy the moment, and be present.

Psalm 62:5 - Yes, my soul, find rest in God; my hope comes from him. (NIV)

~

September 22 - Blessed to Be a Blessing

What can you do today to make another's day better? Give of your time, resources, or prayer. You will be more than doubly blessed in return.

Genesis 12:2 - I will make you a great nation; I will bless you and make your name great; and you shall be a blessing. (NKJV)

~

September 23 - On Earth as It Is in Heaven

I have been plagued with hay fever. Not good! So, I declare there is no sickness in Heaven and therefore there must be no sickness on Earth. What declarations do you need to be making to line up with Heaven's reality today?

Psalm 104:15 – You provide sweet wine to gladden hearts. You give us daily bread to sustain life, giving us glowing health for our bodies. (TPT)

~

September 24 - Tap in

Has God been knocking on the door of your heart? Won't you open it? There is no greater adventure than living this life with the One who loves you the most. Beautiful things are promised for you. Tap in.

Psalm 119:18 - Open my eyes so I can see what you show me of your miracle-wonders. (MSG)

~

September 25 - Run Toward the New Thing

Today, I feel God wants me to leave this quote from my favorite author right here:

"We must dream so big that without the support that comes through favor with God and man, we could never accomplish what is in our hearts." - Bill Johnson, *Face to Face with God*

Psalm 126:1-2 – When the Lord restored the fortunes of Zion, we were like those who dreamed. Our mouths were filled with laughter, and tongues with songs of joy. Then it was said among the nations, "The Lord has done great things for them." (NIV)

~

September 26 - A Joy Overload

Joy is about to overtake you. It is such a good gift that brings healing, hope, and rich relationships.

Romans 15:13 - May the God of hope fill you with all joy and peace as you trust in him, so that you may overflow with hope by the power of the Holy Spirit. (NIV)

~

September 27 - Good Health to You

This is a good day to begin that health regimen you have been planning.

Proverbs 3:21-22 – My child, never drift off course from these two goals for your life: to walk in wisdom and to discover your purpose. Don't ever forget how they empower you. For they strengthen you inside and out and inspire you to do what's right. You will be energized and refreshed by the healing they bring. (TPT)

~

September 28 - Integrity Opens Doors

It is good to admit your mistakes; to take ownership; to be vulnerable. There is much strength in honesty and forthrightness. It opens up opportunity. Your character and integrity are drawing some divine appointments even now.

Proverbs 3:3 - Let your life be shaped by integrity, with truth written upon your heart. (TPT)

~

September 29 - New Day, New Joy

It's funny that God would create such cute creatures as raccoons. You almost want to invite them to raid your garbage just so you can enjoy their antics. Did you know a third of the Kingdom is joy? Step aside from being so serious and enjoy the humor in this world.

Proverbs 17:22 - A cheerful heart is good medicine, but a crushed spirit dries up the bones. (NIV)

~

September 30 - Pay Attention to the "Creaks"

The creaky floors in our old house are sure signs that someone is moving around. Just like those "creaks," there are signs in your life that alert you to coming events or reveal God's heart about something you are concerned about. They can be coincidences or a message from a friend. They can be a sentence that jumps from your Bible or a thought that passes through your imagination.

Watch for signs as you move forward in life. We are not alone on this journey.

Psalm 8:3-5 - When I consider your heavens, the work of your fingers, the moon and the stars, which you have set in place, what is mankind that you are mindful of them, human beings that you care for them? You have made them a little lower than the angels and crowned them with glory and honor. (NIV)

October

October

October 1 - No More Foxes

Today a squirrel chewed down three of my huge sunflowers. So, I made a centerpiece with the flowers and fed the squirrel something better in the backyard feeder in hopes he wouldn't do more damage. It reminded me of *Song of Songs 2:15* and the little foxes that steal the vines and ruin the harvest. God is trying to tell us not to let small things upset us. What little foxes are trying to steal your joy, your peace, and your dreams? That ends today. Usher those critters out of your life and joyfully continue on toward your victory.

Song of Songs 2:15 – You must catch the troubling foxes, those sly little foxes that hinder our relationship. For they raid our budding vineyard of love to ruin what I've planted within you. (TPT)

~

October 2 - You Are Beautiful in All Your Ways

My grandson and I watched the lunar eclipse of the supermoon and resulting red moon. What was exciting was people all over the world watched. They left their busy-ness for a long moment to look up. And those who witnessed it were not disappointed. NBC news reported it as the most watched show ever with the highest ratings ever. Photos streamed over the TV and internet. For one moment, our world was one in awe of the Heavens and the beauty of Creation. May we never lose our wonder.

Psalm 139:12 - ...even the darkness will not be dark to you; the night will shine like the day, for darkness is as light to you. (NIV)

~

October 3 - Record Your Dreams

God will keep your soul in peace and safety as you sleep. That way you can dream without fear. Pay attention to what you are dreaming. Record your dreams on your phone or in your journal. What do you think they're about?

Genesis 41:11 - Each of us had a dream the same night, and each dream had a meaning of its own. (NIV)

Psalm 91:11 – God sends angels with special orders to protect you wherever you go, defending you from all harm. (TPT)

~

October 4 - Better "Vision"

Just as my camera sometimes catches colors, images, and things in the background I didn't know were there, so our minds and hearts are not always aware of everything happening around us. New things are being revealed today and in the weeks to come. Your vision will increase to see those things. This is so exciting for you.

Psalm 80 – Revive us, O God! Let your beaming face shine upon us with the sunrise rays of glory; then nothing will be able to stop us. (TPT)

~

Oct. 5 - A Grateful Heart

Some of my favorite things are still just things. But they open up the world to me and feed my passion for beauty, knowledge, news, and friendship. Those things include my camera, my MacBook Pro, books, skis, and my car. They are but mere replaceable tools to get me to what is real for me. And I am so thankful for them! Today, you will be more aware of what serves your passion for life—and you will be more grateful.

Psalm 107:1 - Give thanks to the Lord, for he is good; his love endures forever.

~

October 6 - Hungry for More

We were made to never stop learning and never stop being hungry for more of life. It is in our DNA. No one gets to escape this fact of our nature which God put into us. We can sabotage our growth, but our nature will continue to beckon for more. Take time now to feed that part of you that longs for more.

Proverbs 16:16 - How much better to get wisdom than gold! To get insight rather than silver!

~

October 7 - Don't Give Up!

Who do you know that is living their dreams for work and for life? What are your dreams? How close are you to living them? God put those dreams in your heart and soul. Don't give up on them.

Psalm 37:23 - The steps of a good man are ordered by the Lord, and He delights in his way. (NKJV)

~

October 8 - Ultimate Trust

I have a few friends and acquaintances who trust God so completely that He is able to send them into dangerous places where they don't fear for their lives. Hence, they witness miracles of healing and faith as they go with God into dark situations. Where would we be if we trusted that much? How far could God take us and bless us? Pondering this will answer some of the questions you have been praying about.

Psalm 78:35 – They remembered that God, the Mighty One, was their strong protector, the Hero-God who would come to their rescue. (TPT)

~

October 9 – Break Through the Busy

Some of us have been in a crisis of busy-ness for many years. We pray to find a way out but never do. We feel stuck, burdened, suffocated, and desperate. God did not create you to live this way. You are made for freedom, joy, and hope—to have these and to give these to others. Ask God what you need to do to be set free, then silence the demanding, negative voices that keep you down. Step away. Ignore the naysayers. Don't look back.

1 Peter 5:7 – Pour out all your worries and stress upon him and leave them there, for he always tenderly cares for you. (TPT)

~

October 10 – Raise Someone Up

Who can you raise up today to be more than they ever thought they could be? We are all leaders to someone; gifted in skills someone else wants to learn. Today, mentor someone. In turn, you, too, will be blessed.

Psalm 61:7-8 – Let me live my days walking in grace and truth before you. And my praises will fill the heavens forever, fulfilling my vow to make every day a love gift to you! (TPT)

~

October 11 Watch for Bright Joy

The little Dahlias in my garden are so funny—like happy, charming little clowns that vie to be noticed. God is bringing something into your life that is like that, wanting your attention. Don't miss it. Watch for the bright joy and humor, and you will find it.

2 Peter 1:19 - And so we have the prophetic word confirmed, which you do well to heed as a light that shines in a dark place, until the day dawns and the morning star rises in your hearts. (NKJV)

~

October 12 Words of Gold

Did you know the words we speak with our mouths are every bit as much a provider of resources for us as the work of our hands? So ... let us speak hope, truth, encouragement, and blessing, and see what returns to us this week. Let our words glisten with encouragement and compassion.

Proverbs 12:14 - From the fruit of their lips people are filled with good things, and the work of their hands brings them reward.

~

October 13 Time for a Change of Scenery

A short trip or extended vacation will give you objectivity, joy, and new hope over a circumstance that has been holding you back from your dreams.

Psalm 104:24 – Wild and wonderful is this world you have made. (TPT)

~

October 14 - You Matter

You sometimes tell friends that your needs, pains, and dreams are so minor compared to others in this world. You feel you don't deserve your prayers to be answered when there are so many who are suffering more than you. Do you know that what matters to you matters to God? Don't you realize how big He is? Pray those prayers—even the small, seemingly petty ones— over you and your family. Your Father in Heaven loves you and longs for relationship with you. His great desire is to bless His children with good things. He's big enough to care about all of us.

Isaiah 49:16 - See, I have engraved you on the palms of my hands ... (NIV)

~

October 15 - Child of the Most High

In the dark of night when you can't sleep and worries begin to take over, think instead about how much you are loved by your Papa God.

1 John 3:1 - See what great love the Father has lavished on us, that we should be called children of God! (NIV)

~

October 16 - Like a Lamp

How do you know when God has spoken to you? Because it will come in such a way that you will never forget it. You will know it is Him because it will have the perfect answer to your situation. God is speaking to you now through some unusual people and circumstances.

Psalm 143:10 – So teach me, Lord, for you are my God. Your gracious Spirit is all I need, so lead me on good paths that are pleasing to you, my one and only God! (TPT)

~

October 17 - Words of Life

Some tell others the world is going to hell in a handbasket, and they speak from depression, hopelessness, and weakness. Others declare good things about the world, and they speak from a spirit of hope, anticipation of good, and power. Our perception and our words make a difference. I want to be one who speaks life-giving words of good. Today, your thoughts and words will make a difference.

Proverbs 15:4 - The soothing tongue is a tree of life, but a perverse tongue crushes the spirit. (NIV)

~

October 18 - The Real Church

Some churches are lively. Others seem a bit strange to what we're used to. Others are full of life and family love. Others are quite sleepy. Still others could use a booster shot; they seem to have lost their way. But church is more than just a Sunday morning experience. The Church is actually the children of God, following His Son, Jesus. The Church is called by God the "Bride of Christ." She is supposed to be about the business of making herself ready for the groom, Christ, who will return a second time. Is the bride ready? Is she open to the things God is releasing on Earth? You are an important part of that preparation. Ask God today what it is you are being called to. He's ready to answer you. He is already directing you.

Isaiah 54:5 - For your Maker is your husband - the Lord Almighty is his name - the Holy One of Israel is your Redeemer; he is called the God of all the earth. (NIV)

~

October 19 - Choose Happy!

What do you do when you are extremely fatigued? When a cold is coming on; when stress has corralled you; when you haven't slept deeply in days; when you just don't feel up to snuff ... do this. Be thankful for what you *do* have—your life, your health, your good days, and your blessings in life. Lift yourself out of the down times with good, happy music. Surround yourself with good, happy people. We are designed to be sensitive to both negative and positive influences, and we are given a choice. Choose happy.

Psalm 25:8 – Joyfully you teach them the proper path, even when they go astray. (TPT)

~

October 20 - The Best Consultant

Decisions are ahead, and remember, you are not alone. You partner with Father God who will give you wisdom if you ask for it. He will direct your steps and has already prepared a way.

Proverbs 16:9 - A man's heart plans his way, but the Lord directs his steps. (NKJV)

~

October 21 - Joy No Matter What

Do you want to have joy even in the hard times? Did you know that joy isn't restricted to just when things are going well? It's an attitude of trust in the One who is able to take you through the storms and break down the walls that hold you back from the great destiny He has planned for you.

Psalm 1:1 – What delight comes to the one who follows God's ways! (TPT)

~

October 22 - Activate Your Dreams

Many of the rich and famous are people like you and me that started out with humble dreams and a heart that went after them. What dream will you activate today?

"Don't be pushed by your problems. Be led by your dreams." Ralph Waldo Emerson

"The future belongs to those who believe in the beauty of their dreams." Eleanor Roosevelt

"Your dream has to be bigger than your fear." Steve Harvey

"Don't let someone who gave up on their dreams talk you out of going after yours." Zig Ziglar

October 23 - Nothing Like a Friend

A friendly chat over coffee will yield much today. A new idea? Perhaps a deeper friendship? Maybe it will simply be experiencing joy together.

Proverbs 17:17 - Friends love through all kinds of weather, and families stick together in all kinds of trouble. (MSG)

October 24 - Peace, Be Still

Stormy weather threatens to hamper your plans, but you can speak to that storm and it will retreat. (This is in the natural, but also a metaphor for a life situation.)

Mark 4:39 - Then He arose and rebuked the wind, and said to the sea, "Peace, be still!" And the wind ceased and there was a great calm. (NKJV)

October 25 Creativity Will Unlock Your Mind

Something creative, like an instrument or canvas, is beckoning you today. It's been too long. Jump in! Create something or just play that guitar. Creativity has the power to declutter your mind and make you brilliant, making way for new ideas and problem-solving.

Psalm 49:4 - I will break open mysteries with my music, and my song will release riddles solved. (TPT)

"You must have chaos within you to give birth to a star." Friedrich Nietzsche

~

October 26 Sincere Humbleness

When in the course of human events it becomes necessary to say, "I'm sorry. I am better than that. I will do better," then say it!

James 4:10 - Humble yourselves in the sight of the Lord, and He will lift you up. (NKJV)

~

October 27 It Starts Today

Like kryptonite to Superman, there are things in life that drain our energy, upset our focus, and make us feel less than. But God's heart is to build you, encourage you, help you, comfort you, bring you joy, give you freedom, and give you a purpose and calling that you will love. Which way will you follow? Of course, you are going to choose a better way. It starts today. Have fun.

1 Corinthians 13:13 - And now these three remain: faith, hope, and love. But the greatest of these is love. (NIV)

~

October 28 - The Commodity of Joy

Joy. It's the commodity we all are reaching for, isn't it? The things we think we want—houses, cars, dream jobs, and trips—are really just a means to get what our hearts are really after—happiness. There is a new train to happiness chugging in to pick you up. It's okay to hop aboard.

Psalm 35:27 - Let them shout for joy and be glad, who favor my righteous cause; and let them say continually "Let the Lord be magnified, who has pleasure in the prosperity of His servant." (NKJV)

~

October 29 - Is It Time for a New Thought?

Is it time to take a new direction? To make a change? Is it time to let go of an old dream in order to make room for a new dream?

Genesis 12:1-3 - The Lord had said to Abram, "Go from your country, your people and your father's household to the land I will show you. I will make you into a great nation, and I will bless you; I will make your name great, and you will be a blessing. I will bless those who bless you, and whoever curses you I will curse; and all peoples on earth will be blessed through you."

~

October 30 - Supernatural Peace

There is nothing like having peace. Peace is the sign you have made the right decision. Peace turns chaos into something that can be managed. Peace can rule over relationships, causing union instead of division. Peace opens up space for negotiation. Peace drives a powerful vehicle that can take us places nothing or no one else is able to. Today, receive that peace. It is there if you ask for it.

John 14:27 - Peace I leave with you. My peace I give to you; not as the world gives do I give to you. Let not your heart be troubled; neither let it be afraid. (NKJV)

~

October 31 - Truth and Promise

Nourish yourself with truth and promise today. It will give you what you need in order to believe you can do all that you were born for.

Hebrews 10:23 - Let us hold unwaveringly to the hope we profess; for He who promised is faithful. (NIV)

November

November

November 1 - Be a Superhero

Do you know what your praise, thankfulness, trust, faith, and hope do in the spirit realm? They are mighty to break down strongholds, slay giants of fear, and send the enemy running in terror. When you do these things, you are a superhero!

2 Corinthians 10:4 - The weapons we fight with are not the weapons of the world. On the contrary, they have divine power to demolish strongholds. (NIV)

~

November 2 - Equipped and Prepared

God, your God, is doing a new thing. He has been equipping you and preparing you for all that is about to happen in your life and in the world. He lovingly reminds you to "fear not." He is on the throne, in control, and you will know what to do. What an exciting time to be alive!

Esther 4:4 - And who knows but that you have come to your royal position for such a time as this? (NIV)

~

November 3 - It's All About His Goodness

Some think that God our Father is angry with us and is a condemning, punishing God. But here is the truth. He is not angry with you. He is your biggest cheerleader. And though you mess up at times, he is there to pick you up and draw you back into His loving arms. Like a good dad corrects the child he loves, God's discipline is firm, yet kind. His love and goodness are what lead us to repentance.

Romans 2:4 - Or do you despise the riches of his goodness, forbearance, and long-suffering, not knowing that the goodness of God leads you to repentance? (NKJV)

~

November 4 - Joy That Overcomes

There is joy today to break through an underlying tension in your life.

Nehemiah 8:10 - "Go home and prepare a feast, holiday food and drink; and share it with those who don't have anything: This day is holy to God. Don't feel bad. The joy of God is your strength!" (MSG)

November 5 - Target of Blessing

Rise up! Rise up! You are not a target of doom, but a target of blessing! Love, joy, peace, and good surprises are aimed right at you today.

1 John 4:4 – Little children, you are from God and have overcome them, for he who is in you is greater than he who is in the world. (ESV)

~

November 6 – Holy Abode

New health is overcoming something that has concerned you. Step into it today. Your body is such a holy abode for the One who loves you most.

Psalm 103:3 – You kissed my heart with forgiveness, in spite of all I've done. You've healed me inside and out from every disease. (TPT)

~

November 7 - Family - It's the Best

Family celebrations will restore relationships in the days to come. It is a time to rejoice and be thankful for the small things—which are actually very big things.

"Rejoice with your family in the beautiful land of life." - Albert Einstein

~

November 8 It's Time to Be Happy

Speak to depression and tell it to get lost in Jesus' name. It has no place in Heaven, and it has no place on Earth to affect you. It is a lie sent from the enemy to keep you from entering into the promises of your Father in Heaven.

Psalm 51:6 – I know that you delight to set your truth deep in my spirit. So come into the hidden places of my heart and teach me wisdom. (TPT)

~

November 9 Risk

A life that goes after dreams is a life of risk—of ups and downs, of three steps forward and one step back. But you would have it no other way, right? Go after those dreams knowing that the God who put them in your heart is well able to bring them to completion.

Psalm 103:5 – You satisfy my every desire with good things. You've supercharged my life so that I soar again like a flying eagle in the sky. (TPT)

~

November 10 Time to Decide

When I was unsure about purchasing my first car, indecisive and wavering back and forth, my dad said, "Sometimes you just have to jump in with both feet." That word had some power for me. I remember his advice even now when I have a big decision to make and I'm not sure of what the right path is. Our Father's answer to us is "yes." He likes our ideas, and He is with us in our plans. Make that decision, then get on with the next thing in life.

Psalm 32:8 - I will instruct you and teach you in the way you should go; I will counsel you with my loving eye on you. (NIV)

~

November 11 - Rest Day

Take time today to rest, quiet down, step away from technology, and sit outside with your face toward the sun. Pay attention to the breeze in the trees. Take a snooze. Listen for the loving voice of God in your thoughts. Write in your journal. In these moments, important ideas will take shape that concern your life.

Psalm 84:5-6 – How enriched are they who find their strength in the Lord, within their hearts are the highways of holiness! Even when their paths wind through the dark valley of tears, they dig deep to find a pleasant pool where others find only pain. He gives to them a brook of blessing filled from the rain of an outpouring. (TPT)

~

November 12 - The Glory of Friendship

Feed relationships today. Make a phone call. Write a letter. Encourage a loved one. Spend time with someone. Family and good friends are so important to our health and wellbeing.

"What can you do to promote world peace? Go home and love your family." - Mother Teresa

"The glory of friendship is not the outstretched hand, not the kindly smile, nor the joy of companionship; it is the spiritual inspiration that comes to one when you discover that someone else believes in you and is willing to trust you with a friendship." - Ralph Waldo Emerson

Psalm 72:17 – In him all will be blessed to bless others, and may all the people bless the One who blessed them. (TPT)

~

November 13 - Coincidence or God?

Pay attention to "coincidences" and signs this week. They are a way God speaks to us, assures us of His presence, and they can help guide us to what is ahead.

"Coincidence is God's way of remaining anonymous." - Albert Einstein

~

November 14 - Another Way to Prosper

Sometimes things aren't what they seem. Dig deeper and ask God for wisdom to understand.

Proverbs 8:11 - For wisdom is more precious than rubies, and nothing you desire can compare with her. (NIV)

Proverbs 19:8 - He who gets wisdom loves his own soul; he who keeps understanding will find good. (NKJV)

November 15 - Spirit of Power

Do you know fear isn't part of what God gave you when he designed your spirit? No. The spirit of fear is from the enemy of your soul. Reject it. Turn from it. Enter into boldness and confidence. Pay more attention to these attributes, and they will become your daily reality. Today we must boldly announce, "I am not afraid!"

James 4:7 - Therefore submit to God. Resist the devil and he will flee from you. (NKJV)

~

November 16 - A Day for Pondering

Yesterday I planted bulbs in my garden, covered them with mulch, and put my garden to rest for the winter. A big snowstorm is coming tonight. It's time to hunker down for the winter season. But just as I anticipate a beautiful display of spring blooms, I feel an anticipation for good days ahead. Like my bulbs are preparing in that quiet earthen place, my spirit is also preparing for what is ahead. Something is about to bloom in my life and in yours. It's a day for pondering and writing.

Luke 2:19 - But Mary treasured up all these things and pondered them in her heart. (NIV)

~

November 17 - Ring in the New

There is a closing of something in your life that is making way for something new to open. Stand your ground. Don't give up. Let hope take you into the new thing that has been prepared for you.

Isaiah 43:18-19 - "Forget the former things; do not dwell on the past. See, I am doing a new thing!" (NIV)

~

November 18 - Vitamins for Your Soul

My morning hot water with lemon and honey gives my day a good start. The steamy mixture is said to help digestion and promote health. I just know I like the taste and the routine. What gives your day a good start? Exercise? Coffee? Quiet time reading the words of God? Don't neglect this time of day. There is more that happens in these times than all the hours of the rest of your day ... vitamins for your soul.

Isaiah 58:11 - The Lord will guide you continually, and satisfy your soul in drought. (NKJV)

~

November 19 - Where Do You Go to Think?

I'm thankful for the little fireplace-like heater in my living room. The room is our sanctuary— cozy, warm, and inviting. It's where the family gathers and where I have quiet, alone times with God in prayer. Outside my home, I love spending moments reading and writing in coffee shops and bookstores; or sitting on a rock next to a mountain stream. Where is your place? Where do you connect with Papa? Where do you come alive with ideas and plans? Let's go there today.

Matthew 6:6 - Find a quiet, secluded place.... Just be there as simply and honestly as you can manage. The focus will shift from you to God, and you will begin to sense his grace. (MSG)

~

November 20 - Encourage the Young

A young person in your life will pull on your wisdom and need your help. Tell them of their greatness and Who they belong to, and they will begin to learn to fly.

Psalm 79:13 - So we, Your people and sheep of Your pasture, Will give You thanks forever; We will show forth Your praise to all generations. (NKJV)

~

November 21 - Abundance for the Holidays

Coming holidays mean lots of family time, preparation, gift-wrapping, and food, food, food. What a joyous time. Papa God will bless your family time this year with abundance of provision and love. He loves His family so much.

Psalm 1:1 – What delight comes to the one who follows God's ways! (TPT)

~

November 22 - Memories Are Gifts

My favorite memory of hunting with my husband is hiking into a spot before dawn, then waiting, hunkered down in blankets with steaming mugs of coffee. The icy dawn breaks, the sunrise colors the snow-covered hills, and we listen and watch, then walk through the trees, looking for sign and tracks.

These memories and experiences are blessings and gifts to our lives and stem from true love. You will remember something special today, too. Write it down or tell someone.

God gave us memories that we might have roses in December. - J.M. Barrie, Courage, 1922

~

November 23 - What Do You Really Want?

Our tools—computers, carpentry tools, cars—are just means to be able to navigate what we want in life, like love, protection, dreams, provision, and joy. Papa God is asking, "What do you really want?" Tell Him today.

Psalm 2:8 – Ask me to give you the nations and I will do it. (TPT)

~

November 24 - Go After Your Passion

Today you are passionate about something that is very, very wonderful. You were created for life, joy, wisdom, goodness, relationship, creativity, imagination, and adventure. Go after your passion. God is blessing it.

Psalm 67:1-2: May God be gracious to us and bless us and make his face shine on us - so that your ways may be known on earth, your salvation among all nations. (NIV)

~

November 25 - There Is One More Able

Remember, on days like today when you feel weak, uncertain, and unable, there is One that is strong, sure, and so able. Reach for Him. Listen for His voice. Take that step forward.

Psalm 7:10 – God, your wrap-around presence is my protection and my defense. (TPT)

~

November 26 - Less Is More

Clutter threatens to overtake you. It's good to streamline, let go of, and bless others with material things you may not need any more. This can apply to emotional and spiritual things, too. I bless you as you release. Less really can become more.

"You don't get to keep what you don't give away." - Bill Johnson

Luke 3:10-11 And the crowds asked him, "What then shall we do?" And he answered them, "Whoever has two tunics is to share with him who has none, and whoever has food is to do likewise." (ESV)

~

November 27 - BE YOU and Bless Others

No one can fill your shoes. And you cannot fill another's. You can, however, walk side by side and help each other on the journey. Your big heart will help you see another's needs today, and because you listen well, you have an amazing ability to make them feel loved and understood.

Galatians 5:22-23 – But the fruit produced by the Holy Spirit within you is divine love in all its varied expressions: joy that overflows, peace that subdues, patience that endures, kindness in action, a life full of virtue, faith that prevails, gentleness of heart, and strength of spirit.(TPT)

~

November 28 - To Your Older Ones...

Be sure to thank the elders in your life who have poured themselves out to you and helped to set you on course. They are a blessing from God for you.

Proverbs 27:17 - As iron sharpens iron, so one person sharpens another. (NIV)

~

November 29 - Have Fun Encouraging Others

Make it a practice—and have some fun—to encourage someone every day. It could be the barista at Starbucks, a stranger at the store, a bus driver, or a child in your family. Call out their gold. Help them to know who they are and how they bless you.

Galatians 6:10 – Take advantage of every opportunity to be a blessing to others, especially to our brothers and sisters in the family of faith! (TPT)

~

November 30 – Smile

A friend's smile lit up a meeting I was in recently. Like a charged battery, that smile changed the atmosphere and defied anyone to try to mess with her. That's power right there. Superpower!

From Psalm 105 - Live a happy life! Keep your eyes open for God, watch for his works; be alert for signs of his presence. Remember the world of wonders he has made, his miracles, and the verdicts he's rendered. (MSG)

December

December

December 1 – Aim High

It's time to be focused, determined, and to aim high. It's a season for forward motion. God is propelling you … calling you … sending you.

Hebrews 13:5 – "I will never leave you alone, never! And I will not loosen my grip on your life!" (TPT)

~

December 2 - You Will Hear God

God is sending you a message today. In fact, He is always speaking to you. Today you will have ears to listen, hear, and understand. Sometimes He speaks through a still small voice. Sometimes He speaks through others. Sometimes you read a verse that jumps out at you. He always uses your imagination He gave you. What is He saying to you?

Mark 9:7 - Then a cloud appeared and covered them, and a voice came from the cloud: "This is my Son, whom I love. Listen to him!" (NIV)

~

December 3 - What Is Your Dream?

You know that God takes care of you and, like the birds, supplies what you *need*. But do you also know He wants to shower you with things you *want*? It's okay to dream. God put those dreams in you. It's a way He can hang out with you as you pursue them together.

"God had a dream and wrapped your body around it." (Lou Engle)

~

December 4 - Inspire

You are empowered today to inspire others.

Luke 12:12 – Simply be confident and allow the Spirit of Wisdom access to your heart, and in that very moment, He will reveal what you are to say to them. (TPT)

~

December 5 - Social Media Spreads Light

Allow social media to bless you today while you use it to bless others. Then leave it for a while, take a prayer walk, and listen ... just listen. Revelation is coming to you from Heaven's app.

Revelation 4:1 – Then suddenly, after I wrote down these messages, I saw a heavenly portal open before me, and the same trumpet-voice I heard speaking with me at the beginning broke the silence and said, "Ascend into this realm! I want to reveal to you what must happen after this." (TPT)

~

December 6 - You Are Going to Be Okay

You see with your eyes, and you believe that things don't look too good in some areas of your life. But there is a deeper reality. Have eyes to see THAT reality and know you are going to be okay.

Isaiah 55:9 - As the heavens are higher than the earth, so are my ways higher than your ways and my thoughts than your thoughts. (NIV)

~

December 7 - God's Got This

In trying times, remember your Father God is still on His throne. We may not have the answers, but He already knows the outcome. We can rest, trust, and live with strength and hope if we remember to see our situations from the perspective of Heaven. He's got this.

Revelation 2:26, 28 – To him who overcomes and does my will to the end, I will give authority over the nations. I will also give him the morning star. (NIV)

~

December 8 - You Will Bless a Friend Today

There is someone in your life who appreciates your friendship so much. What a gift you are to them. Connecting with them today will yield a special blessing for you both from God, who created friendship.

Acts 2:12 – Their hearts were mutually linked to one another, sharing communion and coming together regularly for prayer. (TPT)

~

December 9 - Let Go. Let's Dance!

Did you know Jesus enjoyed parties? He created parties. He *was* a party. There was something about His personality that brought crowds of all ages around Him. Let go and dance this holiday season. He's dancing with you. (In the following verse, "rejoice" literally means "dance, skip, leap, and spin around in joy.")

Zephaniah 3:17 – The Lord your God in your midst, the mighty one will save; He will rejoice over you with gladness, He will quiet you with his love, He will rejoice over you with singing. (ESV)

Psalm 45:7 - Therefore God, Your God, has anointed You with the oil of gladness more than Your companions. (NKJV)

~

December 10 - Decision Day

New opportunities are on the horizon for you and are coming into view very quickly. You have the wisdom to make good decisions.

"Yesterday is gone. Tomorrow has not yet come. We have only today. Let us begin."

— Mother Teresa

~

December 11 – Become Whole

It's time to be whole and conquer the world. What do you need? Receive your healing.

Luke 4:18 - "The Spirit of the Lord is upon Me, Because He has anointed Me To preach the gospel to the poor; He has sent Me to heal the brokenhearted, to proclaim liberty to the captives and recovery of sight to the blind; to set at liberty those who are oppressed." (NKJV)

Acts 3:4,6 – Peter and John, looking straight into the eyes of the crippled man, said, "Look at us!" ...Then Peter said, "I don't have money, but I'll give you this – by the power of the name of Jesus Christ of Nazareth, stand up and walk." (TPT)

~

December 12 - Overcoming

Sun and rain, day and night, grief and joy, cold and warm. Our lives are made up of contrasts. God promises that things that are hard right now will change. You have overcome before. You will overcome again.

"It will all be okay in the end. If it is not okay, it is not the end."
Kris Vallotton

~

December 13 – Open Doors

Heartfelt thankfulness will open doors that seemed impossible to open before.

Psalm 106:1 - Give thanks to the Lord, for He is good; his love endures forever. (NIV)

~

December 14 – Right Place, Right Time

Like a fish in the sea, you are especially adapted to where you are in life right now. Look around. What skills do you have to contribute to your community or realm of influence?

Proverbs 11:25-26 - Whoever brings blessing will be enriched, and one who waters will himself be watered. The people curse him who holds back grain, but a blessing is on the head of him who sells it. (ESV)

~

December 15 - Happy Guffaw Day

Laughter is today's word. The kind that comes from a baby; from silliness; from no place at all. Laughter heals, is contagious, and is a precious gift.

Psalm 16:11 - You make known to me the path of life; in your presence there is fullness of joy; at your right hand are pleasures forevermore. (ESV)

~

December 16 - Keep Learning

You have a skill set that makes you uniquely you. Learning even newer skills will help you navigate your present challenges.

Proverbs 1:5 - Let the wise listen and add to their learning... (NIV)

~

December 17 - Be the Gift

You *are* a gift to the world. You *bring* a gift to the world: Jesus in you, the hope of glory.

(Read Colossians 1 today and be blessed.)

Colossians 1:27 – To them God has chosen to make known among the Gentiles the glorious riches of this mystery, which is Christ in you, the hope of glory. (NIV)

~

December 18 - Making Memories

A cozy fire. A warm blanket. A steaming mug of cocoa. Just the thoughts drum up good memories. There are new memories being made now.

"Sometimes you will never know the value of something, until it becomes a memory." Dr. Seuss

~

December 19 - Twinkle

Mirth, bliss, and joy. You twinkle with them all when you laugh and love. Everyone is blessed by the light within you.

Psalm 43:3 – Pour into me the brightness of your daybreak! Pour into me your rays of revelation-truth! Let them comfort and gently lead me onto the shining path, showing the way into your burning presence, into your many sanctuaries of holiness. (TPT)

~

December 20 - Love's the Word

Love is the word for today—deep love that surpasses fear. When that love comes for you, receive it. Believe it. It is better than you think.

Song of Songs 3:4 – I found the one my heart loves. (NIV)

~

December 21 - You Are Royalty

Do you know you are royal? You are the child of a King. That King came humbly to Earth to show us how to live. His way brings freedom and joy. You'll understand the authority you have and the resources available to you if you just ask God.

Matthew 7:7 - "Ask and it will be given to you; seek and you will find; knock and the door will be opened to you." (NIV)

~

December 22 - Go After Those Impossible Dreams

What impossible dream do you have trouble letting go of? Well, don't let go. God is in charge of the impossible. Write those dreams down by January 1 and see what happens in the coming year.

Mark 9:23 - "Everything is possible for one who believes." (NIV)

~

December 23 - The Best Papa

Family. It's what blesses you most. God fashioned man and woman in the image of Himself—Father, Son, and Spirit. You are part of the Trinity as a son and daughter. It's a family relationship, not master and servant. God wants to show you in this next year more and more of His "Papa" self.

Romans 8:14-15 - For all who are led by the Spirit of God are sons of God. For you did not receive the spirit of slavery to fall back into fear, but you have received the Spirit of adoption as sons, by whom we cry, "Abba! Father!" (ESV)

~

December 24 - Who You Are Makes a Difference!

Christmas memories are helping you to see your place in your family and project it into future generations. Be blessed as you celebrate the birth of our Lord Jesus Christ.

Psalm 112:2 – Their descendants will be prosperous and influential. Every generation of his godly lovers will experience his favor. Great blessing and wealth fills the house of the wise. (TPT)

~

December 25 - Merry Christmas!

A King came to Earth because of YOU. Find time to sit quietly, pray, and listen. More is being revealed to you about your purpose and your next steps. Merry Christmas!

Isaiah 9:6 - For to us a child is born, to us a son is given, and the government will be on his shoulders. And he will be called Wonderful Counselor, Mighty God, Everlasting Father, Prince of Peace. (NIV)

~

December 26 - A Sweet, Sweet Calling

As the New Year approaches, it's time to let go of some things in your past that hinder your future. You are not your past. You are your destiny—with a calling so sweet and so important.

2 Timothy 1:6 – ...fan into a flame and rekindle the fire of the spiritual gift God imparted to you when I laid my hands upon you. (TPT)

~

December 27 - See Your Child's Destiny

For those who have children in their life, you're seeing more of how God has uniquely created them—mind, spirit, and soul. No one has ever been made like them, with their special sets of gifts. Start calling those gifts out and declaring their unique destiny over them. They are pure gold!

Isaiah 11:6 - The wolf also shall dwell with the lamb, The leopard shall lie down with the young goat, The calf and the young lion and the fatling together; And a little child shall lead them. (NKJV)

~

December 28 – Be Watching

God's glory will come to you today in special ways through nature.

Psalm 19:1 – God's splendor is a tale that is told, his testament is written in the stars. Space itself speaks his story every day through the marvels of the heavens. (TPT)

Psalm 96:11-13 - Let the heavens rejoice, and let the earth be glad; Let the sea roar, and all its fullness; Let the field be joyful, and all that is in it. Then all the trees of the woods will rejoice before the Lord. (NKJV)

~

December 29 - What Do You Love?

What is it you do that brings you the most joy? Do that today. Olympic runner Eric Liddell famously said "God made me fast. And when I run, I feel His pleasure." When you do the thing you love, you, too, will feel His pleasure.

John 15:11 – My purpose for telling you these things is so that the joy that I experience will fill your hearts with overflowing gladness! (TPT)

~

December 30 - Go Ahead - Ask Him a Question!

You are learning to connect with God as your maker and loving Papa. If you sit still for a while today, ask Him a question and He will answer you. Trust that this answer —if it is good—is from Him. He uses your thoughts and imagination to speak to you.

"I bless you with understanding how God talks to you and how He hears from you. May you discover how thankfulness works and experience what happens in your life when you remember and are grateful for what God is doing, happily expectant of future answers to your prayers. I pray you will have such experience with God that you can teach others that they, too, can hear Him through:

1. *Still, small voice—like a clear whisper in your ear or mind.*
2. *Audible voice.*
3. *Thoughts—creative ideas and directions you wouldn't normally think of.*
4. *Images—pictures and colors you imagine. These may mean something for you or someone else.*
5. *Visions—in dreams or awake. God will show you what He wants you to know.*
6. *The Bible—Powerful revelation from God's living word.*
7. *Signs—Coincidences, or repetitions that catch your attention.*
8. *Dreams—Sleep time is when God has our undivided attention. Write your dreams down!*
9. *Words of Knowledge—Often these are impressions, body pains, or words of wisdom God is giving you to help someone else.*

There are many more ways God can speak to you. Ask Him to show you." (Chris Tracy)

(Excerpt from my book, Tapestry - The Divine Design for Your Life.)

~

December 31 - New Year Brings a Fresh New Canvas

As you celebrate the end of a year and the beginning of the next, you are sensing there is a fresh new canvas before you. God may be asking you to let some things go to make room for new things. He wants to paint your canvas with you. Where is it you want to go with your life? God is revealing some new ideas to you. You are getting revelation as you read His word and while you take your walks. Keep a journal. Listen for His voice as you go deeper with Him. Have a beautiful journey this next year.

Isaiah 40:31 – But those who hope in the Lord will renew their strength. They will soar on wings like eagles; they will run and not grow weary, they will walk and not be faint. (NIV)

~

A New Beginning

Upon waking one morning, I heard God say, "your face is like a Monet." What a beautiful thought. I'm not at all sure what it meant, but it was like a love note. This is how I pray you have received this book. This is a collection of sweet love notes for you, His beloved. You might like to keep it going and start over with January 1. You may even want to occasionally close your eyes, leaf through, and point to a post for your day. Let it encourage you for years to come. Thank you for reading my book! - Chris

A Note on the Cover Painting

When I asked artist Rebekah Jo Leebens the meaning of her horse painting, this was her response:

> *The white horse was inspired by Revelation 6:2 – "So I looked, and behold, there was a bright white horse. Its rider had a bow and was given a crown of victory. He rode out as a conqueror ready to conquer. (TPT)*
>
> *This verse does not state who the rider is, but I imagine it could be Christ or it could be a warrior who is fighting on his behalf (which could be any analogy of us as his believers) going forward with our Lord fighting for righteousness, crowned with royalty, and ready to serve our King. He guarantees our victory.*
>
> *The white color of the horse represents purity, childlike faith/trust, surrender, salvation, and His bride. His bride moves fearlessly forward knowing victory is guaranteed. The blue on his nose represents Holy Spirit, authority, revelation knowledge, and overcoming. Rust eyes..redemption, courage..to die for.*

One ear turned back listening for his rider's direction. One ear was positioned forward in faith.

I did not create this painting for anyone specifically. I was just inspired to create it.

— Rebecca Jo Leebens, *Artist*

Acknowledgments

I'd like to thank all who support what I do and who I am.

Thank you:

To my family for embracing your writer/journalist mom and grandma.

To my husband for always believing in me.

To my Kingdom Women of Courage, PJ Clark, Vanessa Stiefel, Cindy Eller, and Debbie Hargadine for prayers and inspiration.

To the Glory Alliance for your wildness and being a safe place to explore the mysteries of God.

To my lifelong friends, Liz Germanotta and Francine Carpenter, who championed me through the hard things.

To my Beautiful Word board, so faithful to a vision.

To Nick Poe and Austin Penn at Tall Pine Books, and Elizabeth Maynard Charlé of Polish Point Editing, for your expert editing and publishing work.

To Don Milam, for being a wonderful and challenging writing mentor and brilliant friend.

To Ray Hughes who inspires me to take colorful risks with thoughts and words.

To Paul Young who models true humility and who continues to challenge the way I think.

To Rebekah Jo Leebens for your beautiful gift of art for the cover of *Essence*.

To my mentor, Theresa Dedmon, and Create Academy for launching me into leadership with artsy friends around the world.

To Jeremy Brown of Throne Publishing who called the coach out of me and set me on course to helping so many writers.

To all who continue to read my blogs and books.

To my beloved Colorado – I will always belong to you.

Most importantly, to God / Jesus / Holy Spirit who invite me to their table because they enjoy my company. What stories we have unfolded together.

About the Author

"I write to think deeper and think to write better. Most of my writing happens away from my office; while I walk in the woods or enjoy coffee friendships."

A grandma, flower lover, and photographer, Christine Tracy's happy place is creating from peace and the beauty of nature.

Chris is a graduate of the University of Missouri School of Journalism, Bethel School of Supernatural Ministry, and Create Academy. A former newspaper, magazine, and book editor, she now coaches aspiring authors, specializing in nonfiction and children's books, and is presently a writing coach in Theresa Dedmon's online Create Academy.

Her books include *Tapestry, the Divine Design for Your Life*; *The Art of Writing - An Intimate Devotional for Writers*; and *Essence – 365 God Thoughts About You.* For more information, visit www.christinetracy.com, where you'll find links to her blogs, her You Tube channel, and information about her Beautiful Word ministry.

www.christinetracy.com
chris@christinetracy.com
https://christinetracy.substack.com

crispmountainair.blogspot.com
bssmadventures.blogspot.com

Also by Christine Tracy

Tapestry – The Divine Design for Your Life

The Art of Writing – An Intimate Devotional for Writers